A PRIMER OF
ENGLISH VERSIFICATION

A primer of
English Versification

James McAuley

Professor of English, University of Tasmania

SYDNEY UNIVERSITY PRESS

SYDNEY UNIVERSITY PRESS

Press Building, University of Sydney

UNITED KINGDOM, EUROPE, MIDDLE EAST, AFRICA, CARIBBEAN

Prentice/Hall International, International Book Distributors Ltd
Hemel Hempstead, England

NOT FOR SALE IN THE UNITED STATES OF AMERICA

National Library of Australia Cataloguing-in-Publication data

McAuley, James Phillip, 1917—
  A primer of English versification.

Bibliography.
ISBN 0 424 05400 0.

1. English language—Versification—
Handbooks, manuals, etc. I. Title.

426

First published 1966

Second edition 1967

Reprinted 1972, 1976

© James McAuley 1966

This book is funded by money from
THE ELEANOR SOPHIA WOOD BEQUEST

Printed in Australia at The Griffin Press, Adelaide

ACKNOWLEDGEMENTS

I am indebted to several colleagues, notably to Professor A. D. Hope, of the Australian National University, whose pamphlet *The Structure of Verse and Prose* (published by the Sydney Teachers' College, 1938) first showed me the importance of separating scansion and stress in analysis, and to Professor Ian Maxwell of Melbourne University, whose delightful paper, 'What I didn't learn at school about English Metre', an address given in Copenhagen and published in *Meddelser fra Engelsklærerforeningen* No. 5, 1953, has also been stimulating. To Mr Alexander Porteous of my own department in the University of Tasmania I owe thanks for discussions which have helped me.

J.McA.

CONTENTS

PREFACE

For the past seven centuries or so, more or less since the English language recognizably emerged, English poetry has been written mainly on the accentual-syllabic system which this little treatise attempts to explain and illustrate. Accentual-syllabic verse therefore deserves to be called the 'standard' and 'normal' and 'traditional' kind. If, however, this were an historical survey, we would see that the tradition has not been static, codified, and unchallenged over its whole length. And, over the past century, while the traditional system remains clearly dominant and perennially fruitful, there have been attempts to put English verse on a new basis—by adopting a purely accentual principle, or a purely syllabic principle, or by writing 'free' verse (a term with a range of meanings). These modern alternatives will be discussed briefly at the end; but what the student needs first of all is a thorough grasp of the traditional system.

For all its subtlety and variety in practice, the standard kind of English verse is quite easy to grasp in its principles, so long as the student is not befogged with false theories. Unfortunately, false theories have abounded to an astonishing degree, and their ghosts still walk many a classroom, to the confusion and discouragement of teachers as well as students. In this primer such theories will be consigned to oblivion silently and by implication. The account offered here sticks to the facts, is in accord with what modern linguistic analysis can contribute, and offers no novel theories of prosody (or 'metrics' as the study of versification is also called).

The order of treatment is to show how metrical pattern is developed from stress-variation; to examine the forms of metrical variation possible within regular metre; then to show how the two factors, metrical pattern and stress-variation, continue to co-exist in necessary and fruitful tension; and so to arrive at a notion of the spoken line of verse as a product of both factors in interaction. This account of the metrical behaviour of verse is then rounded out by a short account of other elements which go to make up the physical body of verse and give it its variety and expressive power.

FROM STRESS TO METRE

The fundamental unit in versification is the line. From the metrical point of view, a line of verse is to be regarded as a row of syllables. The metre is the scheme on which the syllabic row is organized. To scan a line is to assign the proper metrical value to each syllable, thus showing how the line in question is related to the metrical scheme.[1]

Theoretically one could isolate any one of the factors which together make up speech-sound and use it to make a scheme or pattern for verse. One could make a pattern of high and low pitch; or of sound and silence; or one could try to fix the duration of phrases, and use these time-lengths to make a pattern. One could make a rule for the recurrence of consonants or vowels, as in Old English alliterative verse. One could classify vowels by 'quantity' into long and short, and make patterns of these, as Greek and Latin verse did. One could count the number of syllables, and fix the number required in each line, as is done in French verse, and in some contemporary verse. One could take the major stress-prominences in the line, and simply require a certain number of these, as some other modern verse does.

The standard kind of English verse is not based on any of these possibilities, though it has something in common with the last, in that natural stress-prominences do play an important part in determining the metre, without being the sole factor. We may begin conveniently with this element of stress.

As modern linguistics uses the term, any syllable that is pronounced at all has some degree of stress as one of its properties. Stress is emphasis, which is mainly a question of the degree of loudness, though such factors as pitch and duration and the 'weight' of consonants may be contributory. The unit which bears stress is the

1 The terminology of English prosody is largely an adaptation of terms used to describe Greek and Latin metres. The Latin word *versus*, literally 'a turning', was applied to a ploughman's furrow, and thence by analogy to a line of verse. In English, the word 'verse' can mean a single line, but is more often used as a generic term. The Latin word *metrum* means a measure, and metre is sometimes referred to as 'measure'; but our notion of metre goes beyond the idea of measurement to include the analysis of a pattern or arrangement. The word 'scansion' comes from *scandere*, to climb, which was applied in late Latin to the analysis of verse into 'feet'.

1

syllable. The relative amount of stress we assign to each syllable depends on the normal pronunciation of the word, modified by whatever logical or emotional emphasis seems needed.

A backward slanting stroke \ may be used to mark the major stress-prominences in a line. These peaks of stress are not all of the same height, and if one wishes one can grade them further, by marking the stronger stresses with a double stroke \\. At times, however, a still more differentiated notation is useful, one which registers the relative amount of stress on each syllable; this can be done by numerals denoting, say, four degrees of stress from weak to strong. Thus the stress-profile of this line from Ariel's song may be shown in three different ways:

$$\overset{\backslash}{\text{Those}} \text{ are } \overset{\backslash}{\text{pearls}} \text{ that } \overset{\backslash}{\text{were}} \text{ his } \overset{\backslash}{\text{eyes}}$$

$$\overset{\backslash}{\text{Those}} \text{ are } \overset{\backslash\backslash}{\text{pearls}} \text{ that } \overset{\backslash}{\text{were}} \text{ his } \overset{\backslash\backslash}{\text{eyes}}$$

$$\overset{3}{\text{Those}} \overset{1}{\text{ are }} \overset{4}{\text{pearls}} \overset{1}{\text{ that }} \overset{2}{\text{were}} \overset{1}{\text{ his }} \overset{4}{\text{eyes}}$$

Generally the first method is sufficient for our purpose, but the others will be used occasionally to explain particular points.

As already stated, the standard kind of English verse does not measure lines simply by the number of major stress-prominences. It does something a little more complicated: *it transforms the natural stress-variations into something artificial, namely, metrical feet.* How this happens will become clear as we proceed.

A normal metrical foot[2] in English consists of either two or three syllables, one and only one of which bears a metrical accent.

Throughout this discussion it will be important to distinguish between speech-stress and metrical accent and to use the terms consistently. Stress in this discussion is the natural degree of speech emphasis; accent is a metrical value assigned to one and only one syllable in a foot. That these two are related is evident, but it will be seen that they are not identical.

Each foot is a definite arrangement of the unaccented syllable or syllables in respect of the accented syllable. The kinds of feet formed from these permutations have names adapted from Classical prosody. The most convenient notation is to use a forward-slanting stroke /

---

2 The term 'foot' for the essential unit of verse construction may have arisen from the tapping of the foot in marking metrical accents. Considering that most poets check their measures on their fingers, the unit might perhaps better have been called a 'finger'!

for the accented syllables and a small cross × for the unaccented syllables.[3]

iamb × ╱
trochee ╱ × } disyllabic

anapaest × × ╱
amphibrach × ╱ × } trisyllabic
dactyl ╱ × ×

The recognition of the metrical pattern of verse arises from our experience of the natural pulsations or stress-variations of the spoken line. Consider the natural rise and fall of stress in Pope's line from *The Rape of the Lock*:

＼ ＼ ＼ ＼ ＼
Let Spades be trumps, she said, and trumps they were.

The iambic pattern is unmistakable, and we scan accordingly:

× ╱ × ╱ × ╱ × ╱ × ╱
Let Spades | be trumps | she said | and trumps | they were |

(Punctuation may be omitted in writing out a line of scansion, if it is convenient to do so.)

Since the line for metrical purposes is a row of syllables, foot divisions occur without regard to which word the syllable belongs to, and without regard to stops and pauses: as in these iambic lines from Milton's *Paradise Regained*:

Or if | I would | delight | my pri|vate hours |
With Mu|sic or | with Po|em, where | so soon |
As in | our na|tive Lang|uage can | I find |
That so|lace? All | our Law | and Sto|ry strew'd |
With Hymns, | our Psalms | with art|ful terms | inscrib'd, |
Our He|brew Songs | and Harps | in Ba|bylon, |
That pleas'd | so well | our Vic|tor's ear, | declare |
That ra|ther Greece | from us | these Arts | deriv'd. |

Again there is no mistaking the iambic tread of this passage as the stresses rise and fall.

Iambic verse is by far the most common kind, and will receive most attention in our discussion. The next most important kind is in the other disyllabic metre, trochaic verse. See how the natural fluctuation of stress in these lines from a song in *The Tempest*:

3 For a long time the habit was to use symbols for long and short 'quantity' —∪ which are used in scanning Latin or Greek verse. But an English foot is not based on quantity, and it is better to use a different set of signs, leaving quantitative notation available for its own purpose if required.

      \\   \\   \\   \\
Vines with clustring branches growing,
      \\   \\   \\   \\
Plants with goodly burden bowing.

determines the metrical pattern:

    / ×   / ×   / ×   / ×
Vines with | clustring | branches | growing, |
    / × / ×   / ×   / ×
Plants with | goodly | burden | bowing. |

Similarly with Samuel Johnson's:

    / ×   /×   / ×   / ×
Call the | Bettys, | Kates and | Jennys |

and with Browning's:

    / ×   / × /×   / ×   /×
There they | are, my | fifty | men and | women |
    / ×   / × /× /×   /×
Naming | me the | fifty | poems | finished! |

In the last example notice that the marked pause in the second foot of the first line does not prevent the two syllables from belonging together.

The trisyllabic metres offer an alternative type of movement which is again recognized from the natural stress-variations. Matthew Prior begins his poem on 'Jinny the Just' with a line whose run of syllables immediately establishes an amphibrachic pattern:

   × / ×   × / × × / ×   × / ×
Releas'd from | the noise of | the Butcher | and Baker |

Further on in the same poem is this anapaestic line (for trisyllabic metres co-operate easily together):

   × × / × × / × ×   / × × /
From the Rhine | to the Po | from the Thames | to the Rhone |

Purely dactylic metre is less common; Thomas Hood used it in these lines:

    / × ×   / × ×
Touch her not | scornfully |
    / × ×   / × ×
Think of her | mournfully |
    / × ×   / ××
Gently and | humanly

It should now be apparent why the standard kind of English verse can be defined as accentual-syllabic. It is accentual, because one, and only one, syllable in each foot carries a metrical accent, and this is determined by relative stress within the foot. It is syllabic, in the sense that each foot has a definite number of syllables (two or three) arranged in a particular pattern.

The examples so far given exhibit in a very simple way the transition from experience of natural stress-variation to recognition of a metrical pattern. This transition is of such fundamental importance that we must dwell on it further, and allow some complications to appear.

We have already recognized that stress is a variable quantity— one which, moreover, lies within the interpretation of the individual speaker. How much stress is required to enable a syllable to acquire the value of a metrical accent? The preliminary answer is that metrical accents correspond to major stresses. But this needs now to be qualified. Let us mark the major stresses in this passage from Pope's 'Elegy to the Memory of an Unfortunate Lady':

> By foreign hands thy dying eyes were clos'd,

> By foreign hands thy decent limbs compos'd,

> By foreign hands thy humble grave adorn'd,

> By strangers honour'd, and by strangers mourn'd!

For rhetorical effect the first three lines are built on the same model. The straightforward even pulse of the stress-pattern firmly defines the iambic metre, and we scan accordingly:

> By fo|reign hands | thy dy|ing eyes | were clos'd | etc.

But when we come to the fourth line, there are only four major stresses. Yet the iambic pattern has become so securely established that we automatically accord the rather unemphatic word 'and' a metrical accent:

> By stran|gers ho|nour'd and | by stran|gers mourn'd |

It we look at this unemphatic third foot we see that it is actually a quite regular iamb, preserving the weaker-stronger relation which the foot requires. It is the relation of syllables within the foot that matters, not the relation to syllables outside. A more differentiated stress-analysis will bring this out:

> 1   4   1 3   1   2   1 4   1   4
> By stran|gers ho|nour'd and | by stran|gers mourn'd |

The iambic feet are made up of various stress-values. Thus we begin to see how a regular metre can be maintained amid great variety of stress. So Dryden's beautiful lines in 'To the Duchess of Ormond' are regular iambics, part of whose charm lies in the easy grace of the fluctuating stresses, only four major ones to the line:

> O Daughter of the Rose, whose Cheeks unite
> The diff'ring Titles of the Red and White; ...

And this line from Keats's 'The Fall of Hyperion', an important one in the argument of the poem, makes its point with only three major peaks of stress:

> The poet and the dreamer are distinct,

though the unemphatic syllables satisfy the iambic requirements quite regularly:

> × ╱ × ╱   × ╱ × ╱ × ╱
> The po|et and | the drea|mer are | distinct |

'Major stress' and 'metrical accent' are therefore not identical terms, even if in most instances they coincide in practice. Speech uses a wide gamut of stress; but metre deals in only two values: accented and unaccented. This two-value system is an abstraction from the live flexible movement of spoken language. To satisfy the metrical code, unemphatic syllables may be levelled up, while the most emphatic receive no greater value. Variations in stress-value help to give lines their life and energy; they have logical significance as well as emotional force. If we read these lines from Gay's 'To a Lady, on her Passion for Old China' with the proper emphases, we see that some stresses are especially prominent, though the metre treats them all alike:

> And woman's not like China sold,
> But cheaper grows in growing old.

In trochaic verse the same difference exists between the two-value metrical pattern and the variable amounts of stress which can satisfy its requirements. The logical structure of these lines from Shakespeare's 'The Phoenix and the Turtle' requires careful differentiation of the degree of stress given to the syllables that bear the metrical accent:

```
  3    1      4      1    3    1    4
Truth may | seem but | cannot | be |
  3   1      4     1    2    1    4
Beauty | brag but | 'tis not | she |
```

It will be noted, incidentally, that in these lines the last foot is defective. It is a regular privilege of trochaic verse to omit the unaccented last syllable—amongst other things it enables the poet to use one-syllable rhymes. Such lines are called by the unnecessarily formidable term 'catalectic' (lacking) while the completed line is called 'acatalectic' (not-lacking).

Trochaic verse in fact relies a good deal on the ability of metre to make do with rather unemphatic syllables, as we see in these lines from the eighteenth-century poet John Cunningham's 'Day: a Pastoral':

```
           / ×
Trudging | as the | plowmen go
    / ×
To the | smoking hamlet bound

Giant-like their shadows grow,
                / ×
Lengthen'd | o'er the | level ground.
```

It is also true that trochaic verse does not always impose itself immediately with unmistakable firmness. Some lines can seem rather indeterminate until the trochaic pattern of the whole passage is recognized, after which the words take on a more determinate shape.[4] These first two lines of Herrick's epitaph for Ben Jonson could seem indeterminate and rather doggerelish:

```
      \                \
Here lyes Jonson with the rest
      \                \
Of the Poets; but the Best.
```

But the next two lines declare themselves firmly as trochaic, especially by the stronger stresses on the initial syllables:

```
     \       \      \        \
Reader, wo'dst thou more have known?
    \      \     \       \
Aske his Story, not this Stone.
```

Another example is the song in John Ford's *The Broken Heart*, whose trochaic pattern may not emerge quite clearly on casual

---

4 This is in fact true of some iambic verse also, but not as frequently as of trochaics.

reading, for two reasons: some of the first syllables are not very emphatic; and the sense-grouping of the words in some lines cuts across the trochaic pattern and suggests an iambic one. Nevertheless the scansion is quite clear as we divide the line into feet:

> Oh no | more, no | more, too | late |
> Sighes are | spent; the | burning | Tapers |
> Of a | life as | chaste as | Fate, |
> Pure as | are un|written | papers,|
> Are burnt | out: no | heat, no | light |
> Now re|maines; 'tis | ever | night.|

This example reminds us again that from the metrical point of view a line of verse is a syllabic row whose feet are marked off, beginning from the first syllable, without regard to how they hang together in words and phrases.

The natural gait of spoken English is closer to an iambic pattern than to any other metres, and this is the basic reason for the slightly greater difficulty they can have in establishing themselves: they go somewhat against the grain of the language. Sometimes there is a slight forcing of the words to make them lean the right way. In Browning's poem 'Before', it is the already established trochaic pattern that ensures that we give these regularly trochaic lines near the end of the poem their proper emphases, which might not impose themselves on us if we considered the lines out of context:

> Once more — Will the wronger, at this last of all,
> Dare to say, 'I did wrong,' rising in his fall?

This need to overcome the more usual habits of the language makes the formality of trochaic metre more noticeable, which also means that it can become an expressive means, part of the very thing the poem is trying to present, as in the nimble and precise footing of Milton's:

> Com, and trip it as ye go
> On the light fantastick toe, . . .

or the long sloping measure of Campion's:

> Never weather-beaten Saile more willing bent to shore,
> Never tyred Pilgrims limbs affected slumber more, . . .

or the admonitory emphasis of Blake's:

> Never seek to tell thy love,
> Love that never told can be. . . .

Of course the metre in itself does not carry these expressive powers: it has a potentiality which is actualized and specified only by the words: it absorbs the mood of the words, but in turn supports and enhances that mood.

What is true of trochaics is even more true of the trisyllabic metres. Sometimes they don't become instantly established at first glance. But when they are recognized they can quickly become rather assertive and masterful, prevailing upon the words, even pressuring them a little, to bring them into conformity with the pattern. I have already quoted the first line of Prior's 'Jinny the Just', which is unequivocally amphibrachic:

> Releas'd from the noise of the Butcher and Baker . . . .

But the next line certainly doesn't start with the amphibrachic pattern, and we may easily stumble in uncertainty, reading the natural stresses thus:

> Who, my old Friends be thanked, did seldom forsake her

before we see that the appropriate reading is one that gives the related trisyllabic metre of anapaests in the first two feet:

> Who my old | Friends be thanked | did seldom | forsake her |

Under the pressure of the trisyllabic metre, the gramatically suspended word 'who' is induced to recede in emphasis, and so is the word 'Friends'. We shall be examining later, with particular reference to iambic verse, the way in which a certain tension can properly develop between the natural stress-profile of the line and the metrical pattern. Such a tension can arise in trisyllabic verse too, and it exists in this line. But because trisyllabic verse is already going somewhat against the natural grain of the language, it cannot be subjected to very much tension before uncertainty and overstrain sets in, and the line threatens to break down. The extreme case is when the assertive demands of the metre cause actual distortion, imposing a reading of the stresses that is quite unnatural. An example is the latter half of the second of these lines of Isaac-Watt's anapaestic poem for children, 'The Sluggard':

> As the Door | on its Hin|ges so he | on his bed|
> Turns his Sides | and his Shoul|ders and his | heavy Head |

Dwelling on odd lines that can cause uncertainty, or are even metrically unsatisfactory, can give the wrong impression that scansion is beset with difficulties.

This is not so. It is by the whole passage that the metre is recognized and firmly established. Hard cases are rare, and need not trouble us unduly. Once the metrical pattern is clear, it goes on in our mind as a pattern of expectation, able to resolve ambiguous syllables in its favour, and able at times to overcome the slight reluctance of an occasional phrase to take the required shape—so long as the reluctance is not too great.

METRICAL VARIATION

So far we have looked mostly at lines that exhibit a high degree of regularity. The most notable exception was the line by Prior last quoted, which began as anapaestic and changed half-way-through to amphibrachs. This is only one of the metrical variations that are permitted as a normal part of the system. Unvarying regularity is not the ideal towards which English verse aspires. The kinds of metrical variation we must now consider are not breaches of the rules. They occur at irregular intervals, at the choice of the poet, but they are part of the normal and expected behaviour of verse. It will be noted that what we are considering here is *metrical* variation: other factors which give verse its infinite variety will be discussed later.

We have already mentioned one liberty the poet has in trochaic verse: the writing of catalectic lines to get a 'masculine' ending, i.e., termination on an accented syllable; as in Herrick's 'The White Island':

> In this | world (the | Isle of | Dreames) |
> While we | sit by | sorrowes | streames |
> Teares and | terrors | are our | theames |

The opposite liberty exists in iambic verse, where if the poet wants a 'feminine' ending he can add an unaccented last syllable. This is not regarded as creating an amphibrach in this case: the syllable is 'hypermetrical' i.e., not counted as part of the metre, and in scansion brackets are used to indicate this: as in Swift's lines:

> $\qquad\qquad\qquad\quad$ × $\quad$ ╱ (×)
> He ne|ver thought | an ho|nour done him |
> $\qquad\qquad\qquad$ × $\quad$ ╱ (×)
> Because | a duke | was proud | to own him |

The main kind of metrical variation is substitution of feet. Any foot can be substituted for any other in any part of the line. The extent to which the poet avails himself of this liberty depends on his own judgment, which may be influenced by the conventions of his time, as regards the amount of strictness or looseness thought tolerable. Substitution of feet will be considered here primarily in iambic verse, where it is very common and quite indispensable.

The most frequent substitution is of a trochee for an iamb in the first foot; as in Jonson's:

>   / ×
> Drink to | me, on|ly, with | thine eyes |

or this line from Pope:

>   / ×
> Such were | the Notes | thy once-|lov'd Po|et sung |

or this from Browning:

>   / ×
> What, sir? | You won't | shake hands? | Because | I cheat |

A trochaic foot in an iambic line is often called a 'reversed foot'. Notice that the initial trochee does not make the whole line trochaic. It would be an insensitive student who said, 'Ah, a trochee,' and then tramped mentally down the rest of the line forcing trochees on it regardless of natural stress—but such students exist. We should quickly learn to recognize the characteristic / × × / by which the line recovers its iambic tread.

Substitution of a trochee at other points in the line is less frequent. Often it comes after a pause, with an effect like the beginning of a line, as in Milton's:

> With vain | attempt. | Him the | Almigh|ty Power |
> Hurl'd head|long . . .

Donne uses it to define the angles of his grammatical structure in:

>   /   ×
> But as | a child | kept from | the Font | until |
>   / ×
> A Prince | expec|ted long | come to | fulfil |
>
> The ce|remo|nies . . . .

Crashaw gets a special effect by two reversed feet, in each case with a slight pause after the accent imposed by natural articulation:

>   / × × /   / × × / × /
> Creeps on | the soft | touch of | a ten|der tone |

A reversed foot can give a ripple, or tremor, to the line, because it brings two unaccented syllables together: as in four consecutive lines of Surrey's translation of Book Two of the *Aeneid*, where an expressive effect is certainly intended (the simile describes the fall of Troy):

> Like as the elm forgrown in mountains hye,
>
> Rond hewen with axe, that husbandmen
>
>   / ×   × /
> With thick assaultes | strive to | tear up, | doth threat;
>
>   / ×   × /
> And hackt beneath | trembling | doth bend | his top,
>
>   / ×   × /
> Till yold with strokes, | giving | the lat|ter crack,
>
>   /   ×   ×   /
> Rent from | the heighth | with ruine it doth fall.

Robert Bridges uses a reversed foot in two of these lines in a way which energizes slightly the verbs that carry the action:

> The bell that call'd to horse calls now to prayers,
>
>   / ×
> And silent nuns | tread the | familiar stairs.

> Within the peach-clad walls that old outlaw,
>
>   / ×
> The Roman wolf, | scratches | with privy paw.

Substitution of a trisyllabic foot in an iambic line can produce many different effects. Sometimes it is no more than a slight passing ripple, as often in Chaucer:

>   × × /
> And dri|ven away | the lon|ge nygh|tes blake |

or Milton:

>   × ×   /
> Of all | that in|solent Greece | or haugh|ty Rome |

or a little more noticeable as in Pope's line, where two vowel sounds are put together, followed by a slight pause required for natural articulation:

>   × ×   /
> The free|zing Ta|nais through | a waste | of snows |

A similar instance with a still more marked effect is Tennyson's:

>   × × /
> Now lies | the earth | all Da|nae to | the stars |

Another line of Tennyson gains a special effect by multiple trisyllabic substitution in an iambic pattern:

>   / × ×   × / × /   / × ×   ×   ×   /
> Myriads | of ri|vulets | hurrying | through the lawn |

Generally substitution is neither so lavish nor so obvious in its intentions, but may nevertheless discreetly support the meaning, as in Arnold's:

> But since | life teems | with ill |
>
>   × ×   ╱
> Nurse no | extra|vagant hope |

Robert Bridges in the first of these two lines has a trisyllabic and a disyllabic substitution with a wavering effect which is subtly expressive:

>   × ×   ╱   ╱ ×
> The | pale indif|ferent ghosts | wander, | and snatch |
> The sweeter moments of their broken dreams, . . .

In iambic verse, trisyllabic substitution is generally avoided in the first foot and in the second foot, because the effect seems to be excessively loose—perhaps for the reason that in both cases the unaccented first syllable of the line can seem to become 'hyper-metrical' as if it were only a supernumerary leading-note, not part of the metre:

> × ╱ × | × ╱ | seems to become (×) ╱ × | × ╱ |
> × ╱ | × × ╱ | seems to become (×) ╱ × | × ╱ |

This avoidance of trisyllabic substitution in the first two places does not apply so much to the shorter measures of only two or three feet. Nor is it an absolute rule. Bridges shows that it can be ignored quite happily, as he does in 'November' (all substituted feet are marked):

>   × ×   ╱   × ×   ╱
> As awhile, | surmoun|ting a crest, | in sharp | outline |
>   ×× ╱
> (A mi|niature | of toil, | a gem's | design,) |
>   ×   ×   ╱
> They are pic|tured, hor|ses and men, | or now | nearby |
>   ╱ ×
> Above | the lane | they shout | lifting | the share |

In the examples of trisyllabic substitution given above from Chaucer and Milton, the two syllables run together so easily that the question may occur whether there is not virtual elision of the first syllable: 'driv'n away' and 'ins'lent Greece'. There is in practice a continuous gradation, from giving two such syllables full separate value, through reducing their value so that they become a 'slide' or 'slur', to complete elision of the first vowel.[5] In this line by Pope, we may accept as complete elisions the first and third contractions indicated by an apostrophe; but we need not be bluffed by the second apostrophe into thinking that we must try to make a complete elision in pronunciation:

> With slaught'ring Guns th'unweary'd Fowler roves

Sixteenth, seventeenth and eighteenth century texts use apostrophe marks to indicate various degrees of shortening or running together so as to make two syllables approach the value of one:

> They looking back all th'Eastern side beheld
>
> But long sh'ath been away
>
> Coheire to'his glory'and Sabbaths endlesse rest
>
> Full many a glorious morning have I seen

The first of these examples is from Milton, the second and third from Donne. The last, from Shakespeare, does not use an apostrophe, but relies on the convention then prevailing that 'y' in such positions could be given consonantal rather than vowel value and thus did not produce a trisyllabic foot. It is notable that Tennyson, writing very regular trochaics in 'Locksley Hall' has recourse to this old convention:

> Many a morning on the moorland did we hear the copses ring,
> And her whisper throng'd my pulses with the fulness of the Spring.
> Many an evening by the waters did we watch the stately ships,
> And our spirits rush'd together at the touching of the lips.

(In the third line, 'evening' is quite certainly a disyllable, though the printed text does not show the contraction.) In regard to these and other examples of what may generally be called semi-elision, it is not a matter of much moment whether our scansion treats the

---

5 The old technical terms distinguish different methods of contraction for metrical reasons: *apocopation* is the dropping of a syllable, including a vowel if this forms a syllable; *synaloepha* is the 'slurring' or rapid combining of a terminal vowel with the opening vowel of the next word to form virtually a single syllable; *synaeresis* (the opposite of diaeresis) is a similar combining of vowels within a word to form a virtual diphthong; or, if the combination thus made is not a recognized diphthong, the process is called *synizesis*. *Elision* is properly the complete non-pronunciation of a speech-sound. These terms are rather cumbersome, and are to some extent suspect because they have been involved in the false ideas proposed by grammarians and prosodists who regarded trisyllabic substitutions as irregularities that should where possible be conjured away by the use of apostrophes.

syllables concerned as virtually one syllable, or recognizes that the two have not quite become one.

We have already raised the question of trisyllabic substitution in trochaic verse in reference to Tennyson's 'Locksley Hall'. What is true of it is true of most trochaics: substitution is used more sparingly than in iambics, because the trochaic pattern does not so easily recover from disturbance.

In trisyllabic verse, the metrical pattern is often adhered to with little variation; but free substitution is also possible, and poets have availed themselves of this freedom in various ways. We have already noted that trisyllabic feet combine easily to give a sort of generalized trisyllabic metre. In addition disyllabic feet can be freely introduced; as in this line by Charles Wolfe:

> × × ╱ × ╱ × × ╱ × × ╱
> Not a drum | was heard | not a fu|neral note |

and these by Swinburne:

> × × ╱ × ╱ × × ╱ × ╱ ×
> When the hounds | of Spring | are on win|ter's traces |
> × ╱ × × ╱ × ╱ × × ╱
> The mother | of months | in meadow | and plain |

(Since trisyllabic lines are frequently catalectic, the last foot of the last line can also be regarded as a defective amphibrach.) In such mixed verse, with multiple substitutions, it can become doubtful whether we are dealing with a trisyllabic metre with frequent disyllabic substitutions or the other way round. One effect of this mixed pattern is that the foot divisions become somewhat arbitrary: the line can be divided up in alternative ways. Thus the last line by Swinburne quoted above can also be resolved as follows:

> The mother | of months in | meadow and | plain |

or:

> The mo|ther of months | in mea|dow and plain |

Mixed verse of this kind was thoroughly explored for its expressive possibilities by poets in the second half of the nineteenth century. In their hands it seems to be moving towards—though it has not arrived at—a purely accentual metre, in which there are no 'feet' but simply a fixed number of accents, with an indefinite number of unaccented syllables. Christina Rossetti has a poem of neglected merit called 'Last Night', in which the colloquial phrases of the speaker are fitted into a tetrameter trisyllabic line with disyllabic variations. It will be noticed, however, that some of these lines, taken by themselves, could naturally be read in more than one way:

```
       ×   ╱   ×      ×   ╱    ×     ╱    ×  ×   ╱
Where were you | last night? | I watched | at the gate; |
     ×  ╱     ×    ╱ ×   ×    ╱      ×      ╱
I went | down early, | I stayed | down late. |
       ×   ×    ╱   ×    ╱   ×   ×    ╱   ×    ╱
Were you snug | at home, | I should like | to know, |
      ×   ×    ╱   ×  ×   ╱    ×     ╱    ×    ╱
Or were you | in the cop|pice wheed|ling Kate? |
```

Another means of obtaining variety that comes under the heading of metrical variation is change of line-length. Lines are classified as to length by the number of feet in them, and the names used in classical prosody are generally adopted: monometer, dimeter, trimeter, tetrameter, pentameter, hexameter, heptameter, octameter. The seventeenth-century poet George Wither wrote a poem whose only virtue is that each stanza displays the first seven iambic measures in rising order:

Ah Me!   1

Am I the Swaine   2

That late from sorrow free   3

Did all the cares on earth disdaine?   4

And still untoucht, as at some safer games   5

Play'd with the burning coals of Love, and Beauties flames,   6

Was't I, could dive, and sound each passions secret depths at will? 7

Literary language contains traces of another way of classifying lines, by the standard number of syllables they contain, i.e. ignoring catalectic lines and trisyllabic substitutions and hypermetrical syllables. Thus Nashe spoke of the iambic pentameter as 'a drumming decasyllabon'. Another popular Tudor measure was the iambic heptameter, which, as then used, we find tedious: it was called a 'fourteener'. The old name for the common 'ballad measure'—a stanza of four lines composed of iambic tetrameters and trimeters in alternation—was 'eights-and-sixes'. Iambic tetrameter lines are still sometimes referred to as 'octosyllabics'. These names all date from a time when the principles of English metre had not been formulated satisfactorily; they suggest that the number of syllables is the essential feature of our verse, and that the number in each line is fixed, neither of which is true.

Metrical variation by different line-lengths is most often in accordance with some fixed rule the poet has adopted. This does not always result in stanza-forms. One sort of continuous variation is the old lolloping 'poulter's measure'[6] too dearly loved by early

---

6 From the varying numbers of eggs that a poult(er)er would supply as a dozen. Cf. a 'baker's dozen', which was thirteen.

Tudor poets. It consisted of a six-feet iambic line followed by a seven-feet iambic line (twelves and fourteeners), as in Surrey's poem in which his wife tells of her dream of him during his absence:

> Another tyme, the same doth tell me he is comme,
> And playing wheare I shall hym fynd with T. his lytle sonne.
> So forthe I goe apace, to see that lyfsome sight,
> And with a kysse me thinckes I say, 'Now well come home, my knight'.

Other such combinations have been tried, but English poetry has developed a decided preference for a line of unvarying length, usually the pentameter, for non-stanzaic composition.

Stanza-forms may be built from lines of constant length, or they may combine various lengths—usually in accordance with a fixed scheme. We have already mentioned 'ballad' or 'common' measure, which is a quatrain of alternating tetrameters and trimeters:

> O little did my mother ken,
> The day she cradled me,
> The lands I was to travel in
> Or the death I was to die!

These four lines can also be regarded as really a couplet of iambic heptameters ('fourteeners'), subdivided to make four lines; in the sixteenth century the same poem might appear in couplet or quatrain form at the printer's or editor's pleasure. Nevertheless, 'fourteeners' dropped out of favour as a metre for common use, while 'ballad metre' remained a favourite mould for lyrical poetry: an interesting example of the real difference made by the concept of the line. As soon as we convert 'ballad metre' back into 'fourteeners' we find it hard not to fall into an over-insistent sing-song rhythm, which poet and reader both can more easily avoid in the quatrain form.

While the most usual practice of poets has been to keep a constant line-length in a poem, or else to vary it in accordance with a fixed scheme, it would be going rather too far to say that cases of irregular variation of line-length lie outside the norm. Between the time of Spenser and Milton, poets were influenced by the Italian canzone to write 'madrigals' (not always as words for singing) with irregular variation of line-length; and the very fine and exceptional use of occasional short lines by Spenser in his 'Epithalamion' and by Milton in his 'Lycidas' is probably related to this. Then in the second part of the seventeenth century the fashion for writing irregular 'Pindaric' odes as a deliberate departure from the norm became established as a special kind of writing—thus admitted as a department of the norm; and this, continuing through the eighteenth century, was transformed by the Romantics into such irregular performances as Wordsworth's 'Immortality' ode and Coleridge's 'Kubla Khan'. The prosodic restlessness of the second half of the nineteenth century included further exploration of this kind of verse, which has continued in the twentieth century.

One further type of metrical variation may be mentioned: change of metre within a composition. Metrical instability is one aspect of 'Pindaric' wildness; it appears in a different way in Tennyson's *Maud*; it is a characteristic of the work of T. S. Eliot. But the most interesting and successful examples of change of metre within a poem are those to be found in song-lyrics. Campion makes an effective change from trochaic to iambic metre in the third line of each tercet of his remarkable song on the passing of Queen Elizabeth:

> Where are | all thy | beauties | now, all | harts en |chayning? |
> Whither | are thy | flatt'rers | gone with | all their | fayning? |
> All fled; | and thou | alone | still here | remayning. |

Dryden weaves several metres skilfully together in 'The Secular Masque' by which at the end of his life he crowned his work in the lyrical mode. Blake's 'Night', so different in spirit, may well owe its form to Dryden's example: the transition from iambics in the first four lines to a trisyllabic movement in the rest of the stanza is felicitous:

> Farewell, | green fields | and hap|py groves,|
> Where flocks | have took | delight.|
> Where lambs | have nib|bled, si|lent moves |
> The feet | of an|gels bright; |
> Unseen they | pour blessing,|
> And joy with|out ceasing, |
> On each bud | and blossom, |
> And each slee|ping bosom. |

Under the head of change of metre within a composition should be counted something which occurs occasionally in iambic verse from Chaucer's time on. This is the insertion of a trochaic line. Chaucer does it in his so-called octosyllabics (iambic tetrameters), a practice which Milton followed very freely in his early work. Chaucer does it also with his iambic pentameters, as in *Troilus and Criseyde* (I. 810-2):

> What! many a man hath love ful deere ybought
> / × / × / × / × / ×
> Twenty | wynter | that his | lady | wiste, |
> That nevere yet his lady mouth he kiste.

It is certainly possible to rescue an iambic scansion for such a line as the middle one by extending the notion of catalectic verse to 'headless' verses, ones lacking an unaccented syllable at the beginning. In some cases, though not in the above, scanning on the assumption of a defective first foot may seem to correspond to the 'iambic' structure of the constituent words or phrases; but this is not always so, and, as we have seen, is really irrelevant. The reluctance to treat as a trochaic line one that occurs in an iambic passage is abated if one reflects that the two disyllabic metres can and do cooperate easily together, just as the three trisyllabic ones do. It *is* just the fact that the line begins with an accented syllable that makes the difference: unless the line reimposes an iambic pattern by the characteristic $/ \times \times /$, the trochaic scansion will prevail. The real proof that this is the sound way of looking at it comes from reading those tetrameter poems that intermingle iambic and trochaic lines frequently. The two metres combine together in a unified texture, but the alternation of an iambic and a trochaic option is quite evident and should not be belied by unnecessary metrical subterfuges. Milton's 'L'Allegro' and 'Il Penseroso' illustrate the truth of this; and so do Crashaw's alternations in 'An Epitaph upon a Young Married Couple':

> They, sweet | Turtles, | folded | ly |
> In the | last knot | love could | ty |
> And though | they ly | as they | were dead, |
> Their Pil|low stone, | their sheetes | of lead |
> (Pillow hard, | and sheetes | not warm) |
> Love made | the bed; | they'l take | no harm. |

Though such variation of metre is much less common with pentameters than it is with tetrameters, the same holds true: the line is trochaic, tends to be felt as such, but fits into the iambic texture by reason of its disyllabic kinship: as once more, in Chaucer, the second of these lines referring to the Clerk:

> For hym | was le|vere have | at his bed|des head |
> Twenty | bookes | clad in | blak or | reed. |

METRICAL ACCENT AND SPEECH STRESS

To scan a line of standard English verse is simple: it is to assign a metrical value, accented or unaccented, to each syllable, and show how the syllables form the feet which give metrical structure to the line. Usually there is no doubt at all about the scansion. Sometimes a line taken on its own may be capable of more than one metrical interpretation, but in the context the prevailing metrical pattern will impose the right solution. Occasionally there may be some hesitation over small points, but such uncertainties don't matter very much because they can be resolved either way without harm. For example, this line in Shakespeare's Sonnet 30:

> And with | old woes | new waile | my deare | times waste |

is clearly (as we know anyway from its occurrence in a sonnet) an iambic pentameter, and good metrical sense is made by simply marking off five regular iambic feet. But one may hesitate, perhaps, over the first foot: a reading of these two rather unemphatic words with greater stress on the first is at least equally possible, to give a reversed foot. One must simply choose which reading one prefers. A good rule in such cases is to prefer the scansion that most nearly fulfils the regular pattern of expectation.

We have already seen that, though the metrical values in a line depend primarily on stress-variation, the metre of the line is not the same thing as its stress-profile. Speech uses a wide gamut of stress; but metre deals in only two values: accented and unaccented. The two-value system is an abstraction from the live flexible movement of spoken language. We must now look further at this centrally important fact, because therein lies the secret of the marvellous variety and expressive power of traditional English verse. Therein also lies the source of much stumbling and confusion in the classroom, unless the distinctions involved are fully understood and continually kept in view.

Consider this line from Ben Jonson's poem 'To the World':

> But what we'are borne for, we must beare

which is a regular iambic tetrameter (the apostrophe between the 'we' and 'are' in the original contracts the words to'we're'). Our ear recognizes the iambic pattern, but it also registers the actual stress-fluctuations as determined by intelligent natural reading:

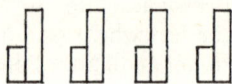

But what we'are borne for, we must beare

The metrical profile of the line is a fixed two-value scheme, which we could represent by some such diagram as this:

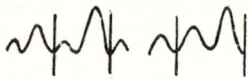

By contrast, the stress-profile of the line is a variable thing: different for each line, and in each line dependent to some extent on the interpretation of the speaker or reader. The stress-profile of the above line could be represented graphically somewhat as follows, with vertical lines to indicate where the foot-divisions are, and a break in the flow where there is a slight sense-pause:

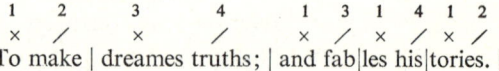

Or take this line from Donne's 'The Dream':

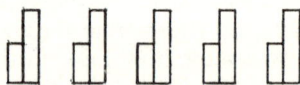

To make | dreames truths; | and fab|les his|tories. |

Again the metrical pattern could be represented by a diagram which brings out its fixed semi-abstract two-value pattern:

The stress-profile would be something like this, with slight breaks shown for the logical articulation of the line:

Note in this case how the first four syllables form a rising series of stress-values. The iambic pattern is created by the relative degrees of stress within each foot, even though the accented syllable of the first foot bears less stress than the unaccented syllable of the next foot. At the end of the line the emphases fall away, so that the last foot is formed of two rather weak stresses (values of 1 and 1½ would be nearer to it).

What we must insist on, therefore, is that the scansion is not an attempt to give a full account of the rhythmic behaviour of the syllables of spoken verse, and in particular it is not meant to be an adequate notation of stress-values. It has the much simpler task of referring the line to the metrical code under which it operates, giving each syllable the value it acquires within that code (always allowing for variations permitted by the code).

But what is the role of metre if it is this semi-abstract sort of thing, not a comprehensive formula for the actual movement of spoken verse? Its role is to provide a fixed scheme, across which the endless variety of stress-fluctuations can play as one line succeeds another. Our experience of a line of verse is therefore not a single and simple thing but essentially dual: comprising a simultaneous recognition on the one hand of the constant metrical pattern (with its occasional variations by substitution of feet), and on the other of the actual stress-profile of the line as natural speech would require. These two experiences are mated, they are coherent; they are not *radically* distinct since metre is rooted in stress. But they are not identical, and a true feeling for verse depends on appreciating the difference.

Confusion about scansion—the converting of a simple almost mechanical task into a wilderness of problems—arises only if this essential duality is not respected. If the student starts to mark the metrical accents on the false assumption that every stress-prominence, and only stress-prominences, must bear a metrical accent, he will quickly go wrong. The surest way of avoiding confusion, and exhibiting the essential duality of our experience of the line is to separate the two kinds of analysis—of stress and of metrical pattern —by making two registers, one for scansion and one for stress, as we virtually did in analyzing the lines by Jonson and Donne above. For ordinary purposes the stress-register need only show the main stress-prominences by a single mark, which is sufficient to enable us to see where the play of stress differs significantly from the semi-abstract *ti-tum ti-tum* of the metrical scheme so long as we remember that any syllable has some degree of stress:

	＼		＼				＼
×	╱	×	╱	×	╱	×	╱
But what		we'are borne		for, we		must beare	

	＼		＼	＼		＼	＼
×	╱	×		╱	×	╱ ×	╱ × ╱
To make		dreames truths;		and fab	les his	tories	

		＼	＼	＼	＼		＼	＼ ＼
×	╱	×	╱	×	╱	×	╱	× ╱
And with		old woes		new waile	my deare		times waste	

More complete stress-analyses can be made in the stress register if needed.

In the last of the above examples, from Shakespeare's Sonnet 30, it will be seen that a kind of tension develops in the second and third foot between metrical pattern and stress-profile, because after an unemphatic first foot the unaccented syllables are raised in prominence by the logical and emotional emphasis the contrasting words 'old' and 'new' naturally deserve. Then, in the last two feet, 'deare times waste' forms a continuous plateau of meditative emphasis with a slight extra amount of stress on the last word. These expressive effects are not obtained in disregard of the metre: on the contrary the metrical pattern is fulfilled even while the 'tension' referred to develops between the uniform rise and fall of the mere metrical expectation (*ti-tum ti-tum*) and the actual speech-stresses, and it is precisely this 'tension' that enables the verse to respond flexibly to the meaning and reinforce the expression. While seeming to develop freely in accordance with natural speech, the stress-fluctuations all the time pay due regard to the requirements of the metre. Stress and metre are continually pulling against one another even while they co-operate. It is this that gives English verse its energy and sensitive capacity to absorb and intensify the logical and emotional charge of the words.

The fact that each line of verse is framed on a metrical rule makes the behaviour of every syllable potentially noticeable in two ways. Metrical variations permitted within the rule by substitution of feet become noticeable against the general expectation of invariance. And degrees of speech-stress above or below what a more or less uniform pulsation of weaker-stronger would require also become noticeable. The *ti-tum ti-tum* pattern is never actually embodied with complete equality and uniformity in any line, but it is felt as a constant behind every line, and every syllable can be measured against it in the two ways just described. Consider this line at the beginning of Crashaw's 'A Hymn to Saint Teresa':

\\		\\		\\	\\
/	×	×	/	×	/	×	/
Love, thou	art ab	solute	sole Lord

The metre is iambic tetrameter with the commonest variation, a reversed first foot. The line receives its strength not from the metre —nor from the speech-stresses considered by themselves—but from the interplay between the two. The main stresses pull the line taut and expressively reinforce the meaning, because in the third and fourth feet the stresses stand in tense contrast with the metre, while not contradicting it.

Contrast, but not contradiction; freedom within order; variety within uniformity; tension and flexibility; the unexpected that nevertheless fulfils the pattern it seems to be overriding; the heightened noticeability[7] of each syllable because its actual behaviour is upon a basis of regular expectation; the reconciling of the natural and the artificial in the dance of language; the sensitive response to logical and emotional nuance—these are the reasons that have made accentual-syllabic verse one of the great inventions of Western culture, and have enabled its usefulness to endure over many centuries.

It is not to be expected that every line of verse will exhibit a correspondence between its metrical and stress behaviour and its total expressiveness so obvious as to lend itself to explicit demonstration. Nor would one wish to see such analyses pushed too minutely and relentlessly in critical commentaries—as with other kinds of explication, enough is enough. But many lines do lend themselves to our present purpose of showing how the duality of the traditional line becomes an expressive resource, supporting and intensifying what is being said. The mere fact that major stresses can pile up in a line in greater number than the metre requires, as in Milton's:

> Ore bog or steep, through strait, rough, dense, or rare

or can be fewer than the normal coincidence of major stress and metrical accent would lead one to expect, as in Milton's:

> Of Sericana, where Chineses drive

---

7 Cf. Yvor Winters' phrase 'fine perceptivity' in his masterly summation of the virtues of traditional metre in *In Defense of Reason*, London 1960, pp. 149-50.

has an effect in conjunction with the meaning—the first example emphasizing Satan's struggling journey across Chaos, the second creating a medium of unimpeded lightness in which the wind-driven 'canie Waggons' of the next line will appear.

Donne is one of the masters of expressive tension between stress and metre. The sense of the speaking voice engaged in energetic logically-articulated argument which his work often conveys is supported by the building up of stress. In its context this line from 'Hymne to God my God, in my sicknesse' carries seven major stresses on its regular iambic pentameter framework:

	\		\	\	\	\	\		\
×	/	×	/	×	/	×	/	×	/
And what		I must		doe then,		thinke here		before	

The summit of Donne's metrical violence is in some of the *Holy Sonnets*, for example in these two lines:

		\		\		\		\
×	/	×	/	×	/	×	/	× ×	/
That I		may rise,		and stand,		o'erthrow		me, and bend	

	\		\	\	\		\		\
×	/	×	/	×	/	×	/	×	/
Your force,		to breake,		blowe, burn		and make		me new.	

In the first line the apostrophe indicates that Donne or his editor regarded the two unaccented syllables as practically contracted into one by synaloepha, in spite of the grammatical articulation marked by the comma: however, it is better to scan so as to admit that there are still three syllables present. In the second line, the stress-register shows three hammer-strokes of stress on the three adjacent verbs 'breake, blowe, burn', which threaten to smash down the metrical framework in their desperate vehemence; but the framework holds firm, the iambic character of the verse is not lost to view. The expressive force of the line is not generated by the stresses alone, but by these as experienced against the metre.

Browning, too, was interested in accommodating highly agitated or energetic colloquial speech within the metrical frame-work, marrying informality and formality. In 'Fra Lippo Lippi' these lines provide an example of regular iambics firmly holding the apparent irregularity of colloquial speech, and even guiding us to the placing of stress:

＼ ＼		＼	＼	＼
× /	× /	× /	× /	× /
Till, whol	ly un	expec	ted, in	there pops

＼	＼ ＼		＼	＼
× /	× /	× ꞏ /	× /	× /
The hot	head hus	band! Thus	I scut	tle off

And in 'Bishop Blougram's Apology' are these lines, in which, as in the above example, the metre not only contains the colloquial speech but also guides us to the proper stresses:

＼	＼	＼
/	× /	× /
Do	then-act	away!

＼	＼	＼	＼
× /	× /	× /	× × /	× /
'Tis there	I'm on	the watch	for you! How	one acts

＼ ＼		＼	＼	＼
× /	× /	× /	× /	× /
Is, both	of us	agree,	our chief	concern

Notice how the first syllable of that last line stands suspended, its metrical value undetermined until the next phrase is spoken. Many examples could be quoted of the play that poets make with the first syllable while keeping to an iambic pattern. Two are given here, the first from Pope:

> Shut, shut the door, good John! fatigu'd, I said

and the second from Browning:

> Once—never mind where, how, why, when,—once say

In the next example, from Milton, the word 'ply' stands out expressively because of the slight break that natural speech requires between it and the next syllable:

> they on | the tra|ding flood |
> Through the | wide E|thio|pian to | the Cape |
> Ply stem|ming night|ly towards | the Pole.|

The vital tension we have observed between stress and metre in iambic verse is not absent from verse in other metres, though, as we have already noted, these do not offer the poet the same width of freedom as iambic verse does, because the underlying sense of metrical pattern can be more readily lost if too much strain is put on them. Here is a small example from Campion of a trochaic line in which an unaccented syllable carries expressive stress:

\		\	\			\
/ ×	/	×	/	×	/	
Tell the	long hours	at your	door

Similarly Shelley in 'The Skylark' draws out and intensifies these trochaic lines:

		\	\	\
/	×	/	×	/ ×
Whose in	tense lamp	narrows

	\	\	\
/ ×	/	×	/
In the	white dawn	clear

We have already encountered the tension between natural speech and metrical pattern in trisyllabic metres, and noted that, while the metre can, when once established, exercise a certain sway over the fluctuations of stress, there is a limit after which confusion or unnatural forcing of the rhythm sets in. However in these lines of Prior, natural stress competes with metre but manages to come to terms with it:

> × / × × / × × / × × /
> Dear Cloe,| how blubber'd | is that pret|ty face? |
> × / × × / × × / × × /
> Thy cheek all | on Fire, and | Thy Hair all | uncurl'd |
> × × / × × / × × / × × /
> Pr'ythee quit | this Caprice; | and (as old | Falstaff says) |
> × × / × × / × × / × × /
> Let us e'en | talk a lit|tle like Folks | of this World.|

Throughout this discussion the premise has been that the tension that develops between metre and stress does not become a contradiction. It is as well to make this explicit, because students can become so over-persuaded of the distinction between metre and stress that they insouciantly allow scansion to contradict the stress-profile. If the reader looks over the examples so far given, he will see that two things hold true: (a) most of the major stresses do in fact coincide with a metrical accent, and most of the metrical accents coincide with a major stress; (b) there is no case in which there is a contradiction in this form:

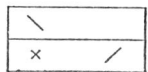

Such a case would simply mean that the scansion was wrong, the foot being a trochee, not an iamb.[8]

Another point that should be made explicit is that the lower of the two registers we have recommended for use in analyzing the line is a *scansion* register, which means that it records metrical variations, such as substituted feet. One could, if one wished, go further, and add below the line a register showing the strict metrical base—the basic

---

8 Having said this, we should perhaps add a footnote on a curious set of instances in which a contradiction does at least seem to occur. One example of the third foot in this line by Christopher Smart:

Bless ye | the nose|gay in | the vale|

The word 'nosegay' has two strong syllables and though the second syllable is a little weaker than the first, it is certainly stronger than the syllable 'in'. Yet one is reluctant to mark the foot as a trochee: the sense of iambic pattern somehow persists. Similar instances are the fourth foot of Goldsmith's:

To tempt | its new | fledg'd off|spring to | the skies|

and the third foot of Tennyson's:

Than ti|r'd eye|lids u|pon ti|r'd eyes|

To resolve the problem by marking these feet as trochees is not quite satisfactory, because it does not account for our sense that the phenomenon belongs somehow to the iambic pattern. The anomaly seems to be caused by a sort of aural illusion, analogous to those optical illusions that make parallel lines seem bent. It will be noted that all the examples have the same general form: there is a slight break between the syllables forming the foot, so that the ear tends not to compare the stress-values very minutely across the break; the first syllable is not weak and is closely attached to a stronger preceding syllable; the second syllable is weak and is closely associated with an unemphatic succeeding syllable. Because the ear is expecting an iamb, we are not unwilling to give the second syllable a little push forward in our minds, though hardly in speaking the line. After much hesitation I conclude that, unless we can genuinely make the second syllable at least equal to the first, we must scan the foot as a trochee, while recognizing that the effect is unusual.

pattern of expectation, in respect of which *both* the upper registers exhibit differences, as in this line by Milton:

\	\	\	\	\
/ ×	× /	× /	/ ×	× /
Athens	the eye	of Greece,	Mother	of Arts
× /	× /	× /	× /	× /

But for practical purposes the registers above the line are sufficient.

The foregoing discussion should make it easy to deal convincingly with two mare's-nests, namely, the so-called spondee, a foot supposed to be formed of two metrical accents on the analogy of a Classical foot composed of two longs; and the so-called pyrrhic, a foot supposed to be formed of two unaccented syllables on the analogy of a Classical foot composed of two shorts. By our definition of a foot as containing one and only one accent we have excluded these two applicants, and it now remains to justify this exclusion.

The solution of the problem brings to light an important rider to our general theory, one which is implicit in the preceding exposition, viz., that the unaccented syllable in a foot can bear any degree of stress *up to and including equality*, without changing the metrical character of the foot. Equality of stress is the limit-case, whether the two syllables carry strong stress or weak. So in Browning's line from *Strafford* (V. ii):

× /   × /
To think | and to | decide | on a | great course |

the second foot consists of two unemphatic syllables of equal stress, the last foot of two strong syllables of equal stress. Once we recognize that equality of stress is the limit-case which still satisfies the metre, there should be no difficulty. Where the stress values are equal, metrical values are assigned in accordance with metrical expectation: an equal-stress foot in an iambic line is iambic, but trochaic in a trochaic line. To do otherwise than this is to invite confusion and uncertainty, and break down the distinction between metre and stress which we have laboured to establish. It would certainly be a misreading of our experience; for, when the metre tells us to expect an iamb, what we experience in an equal-stress foot *is* an iamb, though one in which the relation between the syllables has been brought to the limit position. So in Donne's line:

× / × / × / × /
All kings | and all | their fa|vourites |

the point about the first foot is that it is an iamb, in which for logical
and rhetorical reasons the unaccented syllable has been brought
up into as much prominence as it can have without reversing the
foot. In his colloquial poem 'Will Waterproof's Monologue',
Tennyson uses italics in one stanza to make clear that the unaccented
syllables are to be raised to the limit:

> *We* fret, *we* fume, would shift our skins,
> Would quarrel with our lot;
> *Thy* care is, under polish'd tins,
> To serve the hot-and-hot.

The *reductio ad absurdum* of the claims of spondees and pyrrhics
lies in the fact that any perceptible shade of preponderance of one
syllable over another must by right destroy the spondee or pyrrhic
and reinstate the iamb or trochee. Yet it is not easy to determine
when, if ever, strict equality of stress is present, and different speakers
will have different interpretations. In the line from Browning's
Strafford quoted on p. 30 the fourth foot is very near to equality, but
one cannot easily avoid giving a slight preponderance to the first
syllable:

>   / ×
> To think and to decide | on a | great course

Another instance of nearly equal unemphatic feet is in the first foot
of Tennyson's line from *In Memoriam:*

> On the | bald street | breaks the | blank day |

But here, too, it may be held that there is a slight unevenness which
would really make this foot a trochee. A similar instance in the same
poem is:

> Ring out | wild bells | to the | wild sky |

where 'to the' is perhaps uneven enough to make the foot a trochee.
Among feet with roughly equal strong stresses, the same hesitations
can occur. In feet like 'bald street', 'blank day', 'wild bells', 'wild
sky', such contributory factors as pitch can make the second syllable
seem slightly more prominent; and even the grammatical subser-
vience of adjective to noun may have the same effect. Clearly, the
existence of two-accent or no-accent feet would be a precarious one,
continually subject to such fine balancings as these, on which no
two readers might agree. Another telling example is in the second of
these two lines by Christina Rossetti, from her poem 'Grown and
Flown':

> One heart's too small
> For hunger, cold, | love e|verything.

The marked foot might offer itself as containing stress-values equal enough to be equal. But look again: the line contains a rising series of things too great for the heart to bear, and the gradations of stress may well rise accordingly. Or it may be felt that a more effective reading would be to let the line culminate in 'love' and then drop away, since 'everything' is a confession of failure to define the situation adequately. Such considerations concern *stress*, with its indefinite variability: they do not belong to the metrical scheme.

The best rule is therefore that there is always one, and only one, accent in a foot, but there may be equal degrees of stress as a limit-case.

One other kind of foot whose claim prosodists have sometimes urged is a monosyllabic foot, containing one accented syllable. The cases usually urged do not include the defective last foot of catalectic trochaic verse which we have already noted. They do sometimes include the first foot of the so-called 'headless' lines which occur in iambic verse. If these are to be scanned as iambic lines, the first foot becomes a monosyllable, and can either be regarded as a defective iamb (the line then being classed as catalectic) or as a special monosyllabic foot. But in the previous discussion of this question, we have tried to establish that such lines are simply trochaic lines: special rules and new prosodic entities need not, and should not, be invented to deal with them. There remain however a number of real cases of monosyllabic feet. The only reason why these genuine cases were not allowed for in our original definition of a foot was that we were seeking to state the *norm* of English verse. These genuine cases are not part of the norm: they are rare in traditional verse, and when they occur they are usually offered to us as evident departures from the norm, as Tennyson does in his:

Break, | break, | break, |
On thy cold | grey stones | O sea |

This is an isolated effect, not part of Tennyson's ordinary practice. So is this opening monosyllabic foot of Bridges, (the accents shown are those which Bridges has added to his text, to ensure that we see the line as having four feet, thus matching the corresponding four-feet line in other stanzas):

Gay | Robin | is seen | no more |

The fact that the syllable has to be marked shows that it is a-normal. It is better to regard these rare occurrences of a monosyllabic foot as an exception, a liberty taken outside the ordinary rules. This in no way limits the poet's freedom: we are not legislating, but merely trying to state what the norm actually is. (The poet is at liberty to break the rules any time he wishes: so long as he gets away with it, there is no crime.) To list a monosyllabic foot along with the others as a standard kind of foot would be to mis-state the norm, and invite confusion: the student should not be encouraged to look for mono-syllabic feet everywhere. If monosyllabic feet begin to occur at all frequently—as happens in some modern verse—this is a sign that the traditional norm is being deserted in whole or in part: the verse is then not consistently on an accentual-syllabic base, but has shifted at least part of the time to a purely accentual base. While such unstable or hybrid kinds of verse are part of the contemporary scene, there is no need to confuse our statement of the traditional norm by trying to make it account for them.

The doctrine of this chapter may be summarized as follows. Given a metrical pattern, composed of two- or three-syllable feet in which there is one and one only metrical accent, the question is: what stress-values will satisfy this pattern? Taking iambics as an example, we can answer: all relations of weaker-stronger—and also, as a limit case, equality of stress, whether weak or strong. Since all spoken syllables have a metrical value in the pattern, and also a stress-value relative to other syllables, there is no line of traditional verse which cannot be accounted for in these terms, without any sort of faking, and without uselessly multiplying technical entities.

THE ACTUAL LINE OF SPOKEN VERSE

We have called the metrical pattern a semi-abstract thing. But that is not quite the end of the story. What is shown on the stress-register is also to some extent an abstraction. When we say that our experience of the line of verse is dual, we are implying (a) that the verse is not spoken simply in accordance with the *ti-tum ti-tum* of the metrical scheme, but also, (b) that it is not spoken simply in accordance with the distribution of stress that it would have in conversation or if read as a piece of prose. The actual spoken line is really a third thing, the reconciliation of the related but competing demands represented by the two registers: verse is neither a mechanical sing-song of words dominated by the metre, nor is it ordinary speech unmodified by the presence of metrical pattern. We have seen how the natural stress-pulsations reveal to us the underlying metre; but in turn the metre once established exerts an influence upon our rendering of stress: the actual line is a resultant, a compromise, a thing *sui generis*; it is speech that has entered into the condition of formal art, the dance of words.

This enables us to say something about the true art of verse-speaking. Fashions in verse-speaking change from generation to generation; and at any one time each kind of poem needs its appropriate rendering, varying from the very formal to the very informal. But certain things remain constant and need stating. No speaking of verse can be good which either conforms too slavishly to the mere metrical pattern, or on the other hand becomes so informal as to break the words away from their metrical frame. Some verse-speakers seem to take a perverse pride in showing that they are not bluffed by the metrical character of the text. They deliberately violate the elementary truth with which we started, that the line is the fundamental unit of versification, by recklessly obliterating line-endings. They also draw from the other elementary truth, that stress-distribution is not the same thing as metrical pattern, the false lesson that metre should be disregarded. The right way is, to preserve the integrity of the line and of the metrical pattern, but to do so discreetly and flexibly.

Failure to give the metrical pattern its due can make us miss the more interesting, more subtle and meaningful readings. Donne was censured by Ben Jonson for wrenching accent, and some of his work deserves this censure: but not, on the whole, the best of his love poems or religious poems. Here it is sometimes the heedless and metrically insensitive reader who makes the poet seem to sin. For all his violent straining of the metrical framework, Donne is usually regular in his metre; and he gives the best sense when we allow the iambic pattern to guide us in the reading. Other strong stresses than those on metrically accented syllables may occur for logical and rhetorical emphasis—the crowding of the line with strong stresses is rather characteristic of his verse—but the major stresses which coincide with most of the metrical accents are important. Without the metre to guide us, many of Donne's lines might be open to other distributions of main stress; but the metre guides us to readings which, in the context, are superior in expressive value and rhythmical interest:

My face | in thine | eye, thine | in mine | appears |

and:

Call her | one, mee | ano|ther flye |

and:

And what | I must | do then, | thinke here | before |

Milton is another, and different, great metrical artist who relies on us to use the metrical pattern to arrive at the best reading of the line, even when the lines seem to have a free movement. In 'Lycidas' the first line might unobservantly be given this sort of swinging triple rhythm:

Yet once more, O ye laurels, and once more

But if we relate the line to the iambic base a more subtle and interesting reading emerges, not exclusively dominated by the metre but responsive to it:

Yet once | more O | ye lau|rels and | once more |

Immediately one notices the variation of emphasis when the phrase 'once more' is repeated. Similarly in the line which opens the last section of the poem the metre suggests a more expressively nuanced reading:

Weep no | more wo|ful shep|herds weep | no more |

Doubtless Milton was in both these lines influenced by Shakespeare's:

> × / × / × / × /
> Sigh no | more, la|dies, sigh | no more |

which also lends itself to varied emphasis of the repeated phrase, which the iambic base suggests, though it does not compel it. The wisdom of preferring, other things being equal, the more regular of any two possible metrical readings may perhaps be reinforced by these two examples of how the ignoring of the iambic base may result in our overlooking an interesting reading.

The best reading of the opening line of *Paradise Lost* has often been discussed, sometimes without sufficient regard for what the iambic base tends to suggest. One reading tends to make the line culminate in the two alliterated words 'first' and 'fruit':

> \ \ \ \
> Of Mans First Disobedience, and the Fruit
> Of that Forbidden Tree. . . .

But it is unlikely that Milton meant the word 'First', however important, to be given such relatively heavy stress as to reverse the foot. A reading in which the central keyword, so basic to the theme

> \ \
of the poem, is given full value, 'Disobedience' is metrically and rhetorically preferable.

In Shakespeare's sonnets we can also note lines in which the metre points the way to the right reading. So in Sonnet 40:

> × / × / × / × / × /
> No love, | my love, | that thou | maist true | love call |

and:

> × / × / × / × / × /(×)
> Then if | for my | love, thou | my love | receivest |

or again in Sonnet 42:

> × / × / ×/ × / × /
> That thou | hast her | it is | not all | my griefe |

It may be noted also that metre often guides us in older texts to the correct stressing of words which are pronounced differently from the modern way; as in this line from Shakespeare's Sonnet 35:

> × / × /× /× / × /
> That I | an ac|cessa|ry needs | must be |

and this from Donne's 'Hymne to God my God':

> / × × / ×/ × / × /
> Anyan | and Ma|gellan | and Gib|raltare |

or of words about whose stressing we may in any case be doubtful, as in this passage from *Paradise Lost* (XI. 390-4):

> To Paquin of Sinaean Kings, and thence
>
> To Agra and Lahor of great Mogul
>
> Down to the golden Chersonese, or where
>
> The Persian in Ecbatan sate, or since
>
> In Hispahan, ...

The reader may wish to dissent from some of these suggested readings, and he is quite entitled to do so. But the main point holds: in reading verse the basic expectation of metrical regularity should be allowed to play its part in suggesting the best reading—though it does not follow that it will override all other indicators.

OTHER ELEMENTS OF VARIETY

So far we have considered two kinds of variety: (1) metrical varia-
tions such as substitution of feet, or alteration of line-length, or
change of metre, which are registered in the scansion; and (2) the
interplay between metrical value and stress value, as shown by a
comparison between the scansion register and the stress register.
The art of versification includes, however, the artistic management
of other elements which go to make up the physical body of poetry,
and provide an endless play of expressive variety upon the metrical
framework. These can be considered under two main heads: (1)
articulation, and (2) the fabric of words.

Articulation
While for metrical purposes the line is a syllabic row, it does not
cease to be made up of clauses, phrases, and words. The line is
thus not just a run of syllables, but is articulated, i.e. jointed, in
several ways. Endlessly various examples can be given; as in Blake's:

> So I piped: he wept to hear

and Pope's;

> And loves you best of all things—but his horse

and this from Marlowe:

> Come thither. As she spake this, her toong tript

Such divisions of the line by pauses can have logical-syntactical,
and rhetorical, and musical value. The punctuation may not always
fully indicate the actual articulation. Some writers punctuate more
fully than others. Modern punctuation is standardized in a conven-
tional way to mark off major syntactical sections, and the reader's
interpretation of the line may not fully correspond. In older texts,
punctuation often corresponded more fully to the expressive require-
ments of the line; as in the 1633 text of Donne's 'The good-morrow':

> I wonder by my troth, what thou, and I
> Did, till we lov'd?

In any case a good reading includes relatively slight checks and
breaks in the phrasing which are important for the sense and the

musical effect. Ben Jonson's superlatively fine 'Hymn to Diana' loses something unless we observe the precise articulation which the punctuation in the original text indicates (though modern editors often ignore it):

> Queene, and Huntresse, chaste, and faire,
>   Now the Sunne is laid to sleepe,
> Seated, in thy silver chaire,
>   State in wonted manner keep.

The last line has no punctuation to guide us, but the grammatical inversion requires the voice to dissect it into three parts: 'state' and 'keep' need to be held slightly discrete from the intervening phrase, and the tiny breaks give the line a movement different from the preceding ones.

Divisions of the line can conveniently be marked by a caret sign; as in this line of Johnson:

> To point a moral, ʌ or adorn a tale

If such a sign is used, it should be put in for every major pause, whether or not there is also a punctuation mark

Little practical purpose is served by trying to distinguish between types of pause. In particular, it is not recommended that the notion of a metrical pause or 'caesura' be adopted.[9] Caesura ('cutting') in Classical prosody is a metrical division of the line, required regularly as a structural feature. This occurs in Latin hexameters, for example, and also in the French twelve-syllabled line called an alexandrine. The corresponding line in English is the iambic pentameter, and neo-classical poets and metrical theorists in the eighteenth century liked to think that it, too, had a central division, at the fourth, fifth or sixth syllable, required by rule. It is true that in the iambic pentameter a pause, or at least a 'crease' (as Saintsbury aptly calls it) occurs very frequently near the middle. But even Pope, master and perfecter of the centrally-creased heroic couplet, ignored the so-called caesura when it suited him to do so. And, if we consider the whole body of English verse, we must say that, while the iambic pentameter does divide very frequently near the middle, this is not because of any rule which the poets acknowledge as a structural requirement, but only because it happens naturally.

---

9 The old fourteeners, and also poulter's measure, did have a metrical pause, one regularly appearing as a structural requirement, but it is argued here that most kinds of English verse do not have such a pause included in their basic rules. Caesura also occurs, however, in Anglo-Saxon alliterative verse.

An interesting point about the iambic pentameter is that it cannot be divided into two equal parts even when it is divided into 5 + 5 syllables or 2½ + 2½ feet. The first 'half' differs from the second in a vital respect: it contains only two metrical accents, and the second contains three. The unevenness of the division gives a pleasing ratio, which I hope it is not too fanciful to compare with the 'golden section' in the visual arts. The normal effect is apparent in this line of Pope's invoking satire:

> O sacred Weapon! left for Truth's defence

Certainly the poet can by sleight of hand change the balance of the two parts, by loading the first part with extra stresses, duration of syllables, pauses, and lightening the other part. Keats has some remarkable lines, all regular iambic pentameters, in 'Hyperion':

> Tall oaks, branch-charmed ʌ by the earnest stars
>
> Upon the gold clouds ʌ metropolitan
>
> The blaze, the splendor, ʌ and the symmetry
>
> Names, deeds, grey legends, ʌ dire events, rebellions

It must be emphasized that the articulation of the line is not merely a matter of major pauses. Not least important are those very slight checks or breaks that occur by reason of normal speech habit, or logical-syntactical structure, or rhetorical effect. Failure to perceive these and give them value takes the life out of verse: attention to such fine detail makes each line significantly different. Consider, for instance, the fact that two adjacent syllables carrying equal major stress tend not to run together in ordinary speech but to be separated by a slight check, as can be seen if we say 'High Court' or 'strong stress' with equal stress. This effect is found in lines like this in Marlowe's *Hero and Leander*:

> He clapt his plump cheekes, with his tresses playd

or this in Crabbe's 'Delay has Danger':

> And a fat spaniel waddled at his side

Consider also the articulation required by the intelligent reading of these lines by Campion:

> All doe not all things well;
>   Some measures comely tread;
> Some knotted Ridles tell;
>   Some Poems smoothly read.

(We may notice, incidentally, how the third and fourth lines are varied, in spite of their parallel formation, by the fact that in the third line the greater stress-prominence is on the fourth syllable, whereas in the last line it shifts back to the second syllable.) Another example of careful articulation required by the meaning and grammatical construction is Donne's:

> Good wee must love, and must hate ill,
> For ill is ill, and good good still, . . .

The pauses, great or small, belonging to a line include one at the end, which is never wholly absent, and can be taken for granted instead of being marked. Where prominent rhyme marks the end of the line the need for pause may be reduced, but not abolished. The line, it must be repeated, is the basic unit, and this means that no reading is valid that obscures the line-structure from the reader. It is a mistake to imagine that 'enjambment' requires or authorizes the obliteration of the line-ending. 'Enjambment' ('straddling' or 'encroaching') is the opposite of 'end-stopping'. An end-stopped line is one in which the line-ending coincides with the completion of a sentence, or clause, or at least a phrase. Enjambment occurs when there is noticeable incompleteness in the sense. The mind remains suspended until the next line completes what is lacking. Enjambment may be shown by an arrow sign. These lines by Spenser (FQ III. VI. 42) illustrate the beautifully cadenced effect that enjambment can achieve, with expressive value:

> There is continuall spring and harvest there →
> Continuall, both meeting at one time: . . .

Certainly the usual effect of enjambment is to make us reduce the pause at the end of the line. In some cases, however, the expressive effect may be enhanced by *not* hurrying on, but letting the suspension of the sense take full effect *as* a suspension. Consider the varied possibilities of interpreting the successive enjambments in this passage of Wordsworth's 'There Was a Boy':

> Then sometimes, in that silence, while he hung
> Listening, a gentle shock of mild surprise
> Has carried far into his heart the voice
> Of mountain torrents; or the visible scene
> Would enter unawares into his mind
> With all its solemn imagery, its rocks,
> Its woods, and that uncertain heaven received
> Into the bosom of the steady lake.

Occasionally the incompleteness of statement which causes enjambment is not evident except in retrospect, when we see that the poet

has extended his sense further than we could foresee. An example is
Keats' lines in 'To Autumn':

> To swell the gourd, and plump the hazel shells →
> With a sweet kernel; . . .

where the first line could have been end-stopped. The fifth and sixth
of Wordsworth's lines in the previous example also illustrate this
retrospective effect: the fifth line could be end-stopped but the
sense is in fact extended over to the sixth.

The variable articulation of lines by internal pause, and by end-
stopping or enjambment, should be studied, not merely in one or two
lines, but in large passages, where 'the sense variously drawn out
from one Verse to another', as Milton expressed it in his prefatory
note to *Paradise Lost*, is a major concern of craftsmanship. A speech
in a Shakespeare play, a paragraph of Milton's blank verse, a stanza
of Spenser's *The Faerie Queene* or of an ode by Keats, will show how
important this kind of variation is in building up large, expressive
and pleasing structures.

Finally, under the heading of articulation, may be considered an
aspect of verse which is often strangely neglected. This is what I call
'word-build': the size and shape of the words. Though metrically
the line is a syllabic row, it none the less remains *for other purposes*
a mosaic of disparate words, each with its own length, structure,
rhythm. The slope of the words taken as individual entities may be
different from the metrical pattern, as in Dryden's line in *Religio
Laici*:

> To *lonely, weary, wand'ring* travellers

Where the three drooping 'trochaic' words have an obviously
expressive value in support of the meaning, a value increased by the
fact that the metre is iambic (if they were used in a trochaic metrical
context the effect would be different and inferior). Consider also the
trisyllabic word 'tomorrow' in Shakespeare's line:

> *Tomorrow* and *tomorrow* and *tomorrow*

Where the 'amphibrachic' run of the repeated word is not annulled,
and has expressive effect, even though it is nevertheless fitted into
the iambic pattern of the line. Noticeable, and therefore potentially
expressive effects can be gained by one large word supervening
upon short ones, as in Rossetti's:

> The wind of death's *imperishable* wing

and:

> Sleepless, with cold *commemorative* eyes

The two large word-bulks in Shakespeare's line:

> The *multitudinous* seas *incarnadine*

are obviously used deliberately for an effect. Keats is another poet sensitive to the expressive potential of word-build in his verse. In the first stanza of his 'Ode on Melancholy', a drugged incantatory effect is sought in such lines as:

> Make not your *rosary* of *yew-berries*

and this trisyllabic structure is repeated soon after by the words 'mysteries' and 'drowsily'. Keats also in this poem obtains a balance among the more prominent words by disposing of them carefully, as in:

> And *drown* the *wakeful anguish* of the *soul*

and:

> Then *glut* thy *sorrow* on a *morning* rose

Pope is too attentive a craftsman not to have noted the effect of word-build in the line. These lines on fishing from *Windsor Forest* exhibit a nice sense of the possibilities:

> With Looks unmov'd, he hopes the Scaly Breed,
> And eyes the *dancing* Cork, and *bending* Reed.
> Our *plenteous streams* a *various Race* supply;
> The bright-ey'd Perch with fins of Tyrian Dye.
> The *Silver* Eel, in *shining Volumes* roll'd,
> The *yellow* Carp, in scales *bedrop'd* with Gold,
> Swift Trouts, diversify'd with Crimson Stains,
> And *Pykes*, the *Tyrants* of the *Watry Plains*

Among other features note the way in which the 'iambic' word 'bedrop'd' appears in noticeable contrast to the 'trochaic' disyllabic words preceding it; and the way in which the alliterative balance in the last line (p, t, t, p) is repeated in the disposition of the chief monosyllabic and disyllabic words (1, 2, 2, 1).

Word-build can have an influence on the pace of lines. When many of the important words are monosyllabic the line tends to be slowed down for two reasons. The first is that each word establishes its separate identity and logical function, and tends to acquire stress, as Donne knew when he used so many monosyllables in his verse:

> For, those, whom thou think'st, thou dost overthrow,
> Die not, poore death, nor yet canst thou kill mee.

By contrast polysyllabic words tend to speed up the verse because several syllables run together to form a single unit of meaning, and in each polysyllabic word there is only one major stress: for example 'polysyllabic', 'predominating', 'heterogeneous'). The second reason for the slowing of verse by monosyllabic words is that they tend to carry a larger weight of consonants, as compared with the syllables that are part of a polysyllabic word. But this takes us to the next part of our discussion.

The Fabric of Words

We shall consider the variety and expressive potential of the speech-sounds which make up words. The effects created by vowels cannot be wholly separated from the consonantal husk in which they occur, and, similarly, consonantal effects are not fully independent of the accompanying vowels; but for convenience we will consider vowels first and consonants second.

Vowels have pitch. They have duration. And they have what may be called phonetic quality, determined by the way they are produced in the mouth: as relatively 'open' or 'closed', 'front' or 'back', 'tense' or 'lax'. In addition, vowels can be used with noticeable repetition (assonance) or with variety.

Vowels are the chief bearers of pitch or intonation. While it is possible to speak of tunefulness in verse, the analogy with singing should not be pressed too far. Furthermore, there is no fixed absolute pitch for speech sounds: each sentence will have its special intonation or tune, which will effect the pitch of each syllable; and this will vary with different speakers. Yet in spite of this variability of individual pronunciation, there is a standard order of relative pitch to which vowel-sounds tend to conform: the following words, on the average though not invariably, form a descending series: 'bee, bit, bate, bet, bat, burn, (remem)ber, but, balm, bog, ball, bone, boom, bull'.[10]

When pitch becomes expressively significant in verse, it is usually hard to disentangle the effect of pitch from the other two features mentioned, duration and phonetic quality. Thus, when Crashaw writes his virtuoso piece 'Musicks Duell', he combines all three factors, for example in these lines telling how the nightingale, vying with the lutenist:

> Trayles her long Ditty in one long spun note
> Through the sleeke passage of her open throat:

---

10 I have used the list given by Catherine Ing in her stimulating discussion of the question, *Elizabethan Lyrics*, London 1951, p. 181. It will be observed that some of the vowel sounds are diphthongs.

A clear unwrinckled song, then doth shee point it
With tender accents, and severely joynt it
By short diminutives . . .
And while shee thus discharges a shrill peale
Of flashing Aires; shee qualifies their zeale
With the coole Epode of a graver Note,
Thus high, thus low . . .

Duration is significant chiefly for the syllables that have prominence in the line. In Campion's jaunty lines, using mainly short vowels:

$$\breve{\text{Jack}} \text{ and } \bar{\text{Jone}} \text{ they } \breve{\text{think}} \text{ no } \breve{\text{ill}}$$

$$\breve{\text{But}} \text{ } \breve{\text{loving}} \text{ live, and } \breve{\text{merry}} \text{ } \breve{\text{still}}. \ldots$$

it is not very useful to discuss whether 'they' is to be regarded as a long vowel in the first line. If English verse were based on 'quantity', i.e. duration, it would be necessary to have rules by which metrical longs and shorts would be determined for all cases, even if some of the decisions were rather conventional and arbitrary. But in practice we need not do more than notice that length or shortness can be important. Thus the long vowels in Tennyson's phrase from 'Ulysses':

$$\text{There } \bar{\text{gloom}} \text{ the } \bar{\text{dark}}, \bar{\text{broad}} \bar{\text{seas}}; \ldots$$

clearly supports the meaning. And so do the short and the long vowels in Pope's line from *The Rape of the Lock*:

$$\breve{\text{Fans}} \text{ clap, } \breve{\text{Silks}} \text{ } \breve{\text{russle}}, \text{ and } \breve{\text{tough}} \bar{\text{Whalebones}} \breve{\text{crack}}.$$

Duration of the vowel is not necessarily the same thing as duration of the syllable. A short vowel may be surrounded by consonants which lengthen out the syllable considerably. Consider the lengthening effect of the unvoiced consonants in 'truck' and 'crutch'; and still more the effect of the corresponding voiced consonants, in 'drug' and 'grudge'.

It will be seen that, in giving examples of duration of vowels above, I have marked the main vowels with signs borrowed from the quantitative scansion of Classical metres: — for a long, and ∪ for a short. As already mentioned, these values can be applied to every vowel only with approximate accuracy, and the length of the vowel does not wholly determine the length of the syllable; but this does not matter because 'quantity' is not a metrical factor in English. In the Elizabethan period some poets and theorists hankered after a quantitative scheme, but the language resisted them. Thomas Campion in his theorizing went astray by seeking quantitative rules.

He knew that duration, whether of vowels or of syllables, was artistically very important, but did not see clearly that it was not *metrically* significant. In his actual practice he not only used the standard metres with skill, but also used his acutely refined sensitivity to all aural values, including 'quantity', to make verses in which the variable duration of vowels and syllables is an important non-metrical element. 'The eare is a rationall sence and a chief judge of proportion,' he wrote, and he was able to compose such finely organized sequences as:

$$— \; – \qquad — \; \cup \qquad \cup \;\; \cup \; –$$
Thou all sweetnesse dost enclose

$$– \;\; \cup \; \cup \;\; \cup \; — \; — \quad \cup \;\; \cup$$
Like a little world of blisse.

$$— \; \cup \quad – \qquad – \; — \qquad \cup \; –$$
Beauty guards thy lookes: the Rose

$$\cup \quad \cup \quad – \quad \cup \; \cup – \; \cup \;\; \cup$$
In them pure and eternall is.

Such lyrics fulfil the ideal he stated in his preface to *The Fourth Booke of Ayres*: 'The Apothecaries have Bookes of Gold, whose leaves being opened are so light as that they are subject to be shaken with the least breath, yet rightly handled, they serve both for ornament and use; such are light Ayres'.

In regard to the other characteristic of vowels, phonetic quality, it is difficult to say much without becoming involved in a technical analysis, with the use of phonetic notation and diagrams, which would unduly complicate this modest treatise. However, appreciation of the expressive possibilities contained in those determinants of phonetic quality we have already listed (open or closed, front or back, tense or lax) does not have to wait upon a technical analysis. It can immediately be perceived as an expressive element, along with pitch and duration, in the passage from Crashaw's 'Musicks Duell' quoted above, or in such a stanza as this from Milton's 'Nativity Ode':

> Ring out ye Crystall spheres,
> Once bless our human ears,
>   (If ye have power to touch our senses so)
> And let your silver chime
> Move in melodious time;
>   And let the Base of Heavn's deep Organ blow,
> And with your ninefold harmony
> Make up full consort to the th'Angelike symphony.

Turning now to a consideration of the consonants, we need not dwell on the familiar use of alliteration. One or two comments, however, should be added. It is true for alliteration, as indeed for assonance, that repetition of sounds does not always mean exact reproduction. We use the same letter to cover a variety of related sounds which differ according to the phonetic context in which they occur. Thus there is not one sound l, or b, or k but a range of different sounds we produce in different words: l in 'like' is different from l in 'full'; b in 'rubber' is different from b in 'ball'; k in 'khan' is different from k in 'hick'. Each of these families of related speech-sounds is called a 'phoneme'; and alliteration is really between 'allophones' (variants) within the phoneme. The same is true for assonance. The point is hardly worth making except that phoneticians sometimes become captious, and accuse literary critics of committing phonetic howlers when they speak of repetition of speech-sounds. It need hardly be said, of course, that mere similarity of spelling is not alliteration or assonance: the letters must stand for similar sounds.

Alliteration used to have a structural function in Old English verse, in conjunction with major stress. A line from *Piers Plowman* will show how it worked:

With her *b*elies and her *b*agges ʌ of *b*red ful ycrammed

While alliteration has lost its metrical function in modern English verse, it can have a certain structural value in emphasizing the metrical accents, as in Housman's line:

Be *s*till my *s*oul, the arms you *b*ear are *b*rittle

Alliteration is not, of course, significant only for the consonant at the beginning of the word. All the consonants in the more prominent words (and by communication of effect some in the less prominent words) can be in significant interrelation. Dryden is a master in the interweaving of sounds which tighten his discourse and reinforce the rhetoric. Consider the use of s, p, b, t, r, and then also of l, and f, in the following lines from *The Hind and the Panther*, which helps to keep a politico-religious argument strung up to a poetic level:

But soon against your superstitious lawn
Some Presbyterian sabre would be drawn:
In your establish'd laws of sov'raignty
The rest some fundamental flaw would see,
And call Rebellion gospel-liberty.

This passage also reminds us that 'apt alliteration's artful aid' (the phrase is Charles Churchill's) is not confined to onomatopoeia or the imitation of physical phenomena: it is a constant rhetorical and musical element.

A variety of alliteration sometimes distinguished as 'consonance' may also be noted, examples of which are 'call' and 'coal', or 'find' and 'fond', where the consonants surrounding the vowel are repeated but the vowel changes.

It should also be noted that the opposite effect to alliteration (and assonance) is also important, namely, the significant entry of a noticeably new sound, or set of sounds to give prominence by change of phonetic quality. Milton's 'Nativity Ode' is rich in examples, such as the italicized words in:

> In Urns and Altars round,
> A drear and dying sound
>   Affrights the Flamins at their service quaint
> And the *chill Marble* seems to sweat, . . .

or the splendid effect of the italicized word in:

> Yet first to those ychained in sleep
> The wakeful trump of doom must thunder through the deep,
> With such a horrid *clang*. . . .

Finally, with regard to consonants, it should be noted that they are the chief bearers of kinaesthetic value, that is, of the sense of muscular action—energetic, impeded, tense, smoothly sliding, easy —which is an important element in expression. An obvious but ingenious example of kinaesthetic effect is produced in Dryden's lines on Polyphemus in 'The Fable of Acis, Polyphemus and Galatea', where the Cyclops

> Assum'd the softness of a Lover's Air;
> And comb'd with Teeth of Rakes, his rugged hair.
> Now with a crooked Sythe his Beard he sleeks;
> And mows the stubborn stubble of his Cheeks: . . .

Keats has a brilliant effect in the 'Ode on Melancholy' in the italicized words:

> No, no, go not to Lethe, neither *twist*
>   Wolf's-bane, *tight-rooted*, for its poisonous wine; . . .

It will be noted that vowels too, by tenseness or laxity contribute to the kinaesthetic effect. Pope uses all resources in his description of the sylphs:

> Transparent Forms, too fine for mortal Sight,
> Their fluid Bodies half dissolv'd in Light.
> Loose to the Wind their airy Garments flew,

tightening a little in the next line to stress the meaning:

> Thin glittering Textures of the filmy Dew.

In thus speaking of the expressive, as well as the musical, value of speech-sounds, I have avoided any suggestion that these things exist to any important degree apart from the meaning. It is only through the meaning that the expressive potential of speech-sounds is actually released: sounds respond to and co-operate with the sense. This is also true, to a large extent, of the 'musical' quality of verse. While it is too extreme to say, as some critics have done, that words can have no 'musical' value apart from the meaning—one can, for instance, make nonsense verses that are mellifluous or rhythmically and phonetically interesting—it must be admitted that the musicality we admire is mainly the result of an interaction between sense and sound: meaning is the prince that kisses the sleeping beauty of speech-sound into wakeful life. It should also be added that in a discussion of this sort one tends to choose examples of the most obvious kind, with sound supporting the sense in an easily demonstrable way. But the art of the poet is not confined to such specific and demonstrable effects (which can degenerate into mere tricks); it is shown above all in a general mating of words and meaning to produce life, energy, and delight, as the physical body of verse sings and dances while incarnating the theme.

Some of the non-metrical factors discussed above can be added to the analysis of verse on separate registers which we demonstrated in regard to metre and stress. To make a more complete analysis is a useful exercise, which helps to sharpen our understanding of the

Consonants	h	dj w		k z k i ŋ
Vowel Pitch	iə	u:	ε	ou ɔː
Vowel Quantity	∪ —	∪ —	∪ ∪	— — ∪
Stress	1 3	1 3	1 4	2 3 1
Scansion	× ╱	× ╱	× ╱	× ╱ (×)
	To hear	the dew	y e	choes ʌ calling→
Metre:	iambic tetrameter			

complex variability of verse. In the two lines from Tennyson's 'The Lotos Eaters' analyzed below, the metre is stated under the line, and then, in addition to scansion and stress registers, there is a register for vowel duration (assigning two values, long and short, as nearly as English admits), then a register for the pitch of the main vowels, placing the sound higher or lower, and finally a register for the more important consonants. A simple phonetic transcription is used to avoid the difficulties occasioned by non-phonetic spelling. The analysis so made is neither exhaustive nor more than approximate, but it serves a useful purpose in the study of verse. One notices, for example, the foot without consonants in the first line, the echo-effect in the second line.

Consonants	k v	k v	θr ð	θ k tw	n d v n
Vowel Pitch	ei	ei	u:	i ai	ai
Vowel Quantity	ᴗ —	ᴗ —	— ᴗ	ᴗ —	ᴗ —
Stress	1 4	1 3	2 1	3 3	1 4
Scansion	× /	× /	/ ×	× /	× /
	From cave	to caveʌ	thro' the	thick-twi	ned vine
Metre:	iambic pentameter				

OTHER SYSTEMS OF VERSIFICATION

The past century has seen a great deal of prosodic restlessness, with attempts at reform, or revolutionary overthrow, of the standard metrical system which has been described in this book. None of the alternatives proposed has displaced the accentual-syllabic system; all have difficulties of their own, and all sacrifice something of the unique complexity or variability-within-strictness of the traditional norm. On the other hand, all offer the poet certain possibilities, and valuable work has been done in them. It is proposed to review the main alternatives in summary fashion.

Accentual Verse

The chief line of departure has been to dissolve the partnership-intension of metre and stress: in effect, to remove the scansion register and retain only the stress-register, each main stress being regarded as a metrical event, for which the best name is a 'stress-accent'—the number and arrangement of unaccented (weak-stressed) syllables being subject to no metrical rule. Coleridge experimented with this sort of verse at the beginning of 'Christabel', though he did not keep it up:

> 'Tis the middle of night by the castle clock
>
> And the owls have awakened the crowing cock;
>
> Tu - whit—Tu - whoo!

Scansion of accentual verse is merely a matter of marking stress-accents. The number of intervening unaccented syllables may vary from none to three (rarely more)—but this has no metrical significance. Gerard Manley Hopkins's 'Sprung Rhythm' is accentual verse under this rule, exploiting to the limit the liberty of action offered by it. Many poets writing accentual verse do not attempt to avoid the iambic pattern which recurs so easily; often the result is a rather hybrid sort of verse, hovering between the standard metrical system and a purely accentual rule.

One difficulty about accentual verse is obscured by the habit of talking about 'stressed' and 'unstressed' syllables, as if these were two distinct categories. As we have seen, all syllables carry stress in some degree, and the amount of stress varies indefinitely. The problem for the writer and reader of accentual verse is, how much or how little stress will count for a metrical accent. Thus in W. S. Merwin's poem 'Grandfather in the Old Men's Home', the poet appears to be intending a four-accent line throughout:

> /   /   /   /
> Gentle at last, and as clean as ever,
>
>   /   /   /   /
> He did not even need drink any more
>
>   / /   /   /
> And his good sons unbent and brought him
>
>   /   /   /   /
> Tobacco to chew, both times when they came
>
>   / /   / /
> To be satisfied he was well cared for

Even in these lines, it is only our belief (if it is our belief) that the poet intends to adhere to a line of four stress-accents which finally determines the scansion: otherwise why not give 'times' an accent on account of its stress-value in the fourth line; and why give two accents to the word 'satisfied' in the fifth line? Later on in the poem occurs the line:

> His sleep beside the other clean old men

which reads like an iambic pentameter, or, if regarded in its stress-profile, might invite us to award any number of stress-accents up to six, depending on how we felt the line should be said, and what level of stress warrants an accent:

> '   /   /   /   / /   /
> His sleep beside the other clean old men

Apparently the true scansion is meant to be something like this:

>   /   /   /   /
> His sleep beside the other clean old men

Similarly in the lines:

> With the children they both had begotten
> With old faces now, but themselves shrunken

it is by retrospective inference that we decide that 'With' in the first line must have a stress-accent, and that 'faces' in the second does not have one: decisions made only for the sake of appearing to preserve the scheme of four stress-accents.

Syllabic Verse

Another scheme is to ignore stress entirely, and take the number of syllables in the line as the sole metrical rule. Each line can then vary very much in the phrasing. The difficulty about this form is that our ear is not accustomed to estimate line-lengths simply by the number of syllables. Practitioners of syllabic verse seem to differ in their attitude to this: some say that our ear can and should be trained; others admit that the ear can't easily measure by number of syllables but say that this doesn't matter. The use of rhyme can, of course, provide its normal help in marking the line-structure. The counting of syllables is also not without some problems; there are borderline cases about which decisions have to be taken: fleeting vowel-sounds in weakly-stressed positions ('pow*er*' 'ev*er*y') and also consonantal syllables like 'spa*sm*'. Marianne Moore has written in syllabic forms which suit the dry, precise, speaking tone of her poetry. Here is one stanza of 'Critics and Connoisseurs', with a pattern of lines composed of even numbers of syllables:

There is a great amount of poetry in unconscious	14
fastidiousness. Certain Ming	8
products, imperial floor-coverings of coach-	12
wheel yellow, are well enough in their way but I have seen something	16
that I like better—a	6
mere childish attempt to make an imperfectly ballasted animal stand up,	20
similar determination to make a pup	12
eat his meat from the plate.	6

Free Verse

Many variants can be found under this general heading. The extreme case occurs when prose is simply cut into lines, which may or may not be end-stopped. What this does is to summon forth our verse-reading habits, encourage us to pay more attention to the cadences and the phonetic texture. The rhythm of the prose is perhaps slightly heightened in this way, and it may even be altered a little, if the lines as set out do not coincide exactly with the phrasing but include some enjambment. Frequently, however, free verse moves some distance nearer to regularity and pattern. The lines may be grouped in twos or threes or other sets, with a good deal of parallel or balance and contrast. Lines may be kept to approximately the same length —they may even tend to be organized with two, or three, or four major stresses, so that the effect is of somewhat irregular accentual verse. As free verse moves towards pattern it moves from being *vers libre* to *vers libéré*.

Classical and Pseudo-Classical Metres

It is possible in English to practise a purely quantitative system, so long as one adopts a set of rules for determining long and short syllables. But the result is extremely arbitrary and unsatisfactory.

What does work rather better is to adopt the standard Greek or Latin metres, such as the hexameter, and change the longs and shorts into accents and unaccented syllables. In skilful hands the results are not devoid of interest, as Arthur Hugh Clough demonstrated in his *Amours de Voyage*:

> Ah, for a child in the street I could strike; for the full-blown lady—
> Somehow, Eustace, alas! I have not felt the vocation.

A SHORT GLOSSARY

accent. Like many prosodic terms, this word is used in different senses by different theorists. In this book it means a metrical value assigned to a syllable.

alexandrine. A term borrowed from French prosody, where it is applied to the French 'heroic' line of twelve syllables (derived either from the poet Alexandre Paris, or from heroic poems about Alexander). In English it is an iambic hexameter, especially as used to vary the heroic couplet (*q.v.*), or to amplify it to a triplet by adding a rhyming third line. Pope disliked this use, and refers to it in *An Essay on Criticism*:

> A needless Alexandrine ends the song
> That like a wounded snake, drags its slow length along.

alliteration. Repetition of a consonant; sometimes used to cover repetition of vowels also.

anacrusis. The addition of a hypermetrical (*q.v.*) syllable at the beginning of a line, i.e. one regarded as not counting for the scansion: rare in formal traditional verse.

assonance. Repetition of a vowel; sometimes more loosely applied to approximate similarity of rhymes.

blank verse. Verse without rhyme; but especially unrhymed iambic pentameters or 'heroic' verse as used in drama and in epic poetry.

catalexis. The omission of the final unaccented syllable or syllables in a trochee, amphibrach, or dactyl for the purpose of obtaining a 'masculine' ending; ordinarily regarded as a case distinct from a monosyllabic foot. A line in which there is no defect in the last foot is called 'catalectic'.

consonance. Loosely used of agreement of sounds, but sometimes restricted to change of vowel while the enclosing consonants remain the same (port/part).

couplet. Two adjacent lines rhymed together. If the second line completes a major unit of sense it is a closed couplet. (See also *heroic couplet*.)

distich. A couplet, usually making complete sense and often standing on its own.

55

doggerel. Verse which fails, either through the poet's unskilfulness or by deliberate comic intention, to achieve a satisfactory metrical order.

elision. Strictly, the complete omission in pronunciation of a speech-sound normally pronounced; but in the case of a vowel elision may be incomplete, leaving a fleeting remnant of the sound, as in such expressions as 'th'old'.

enjambment. The opposite of end-stopping: the sense runs over from one line to the next. The normal terminal pause may be thereby reduced, but not necessarily.

falling metre. A term sometimes applied to a trochaic metre, where the foot falls away from the initial accent. (Compare *rising metre.*)

French forms. A number of elaborate fixed forms were adopted into English from French poetry and used by Chaucer and others. In the later part of the nineteenth century they were revived by Swinburne, Dobson and others. While their modern use has mostly been for light verse, they have also been used for more serious poems, though usually of a rather mannered or highly artificial kind. Such are the triolet, rondel, rondeau, ballade, villanelle. They are best studied from examples in French or early English usage, or in the work of the late Victorian practitioners.

heroic couplet. Iambic pentameters rhymed together and usually 'closed' at the end, so named because the iambic pentameter was regarded as the line best suited for heroic or epic poetry, though the heroic couplet found its chief use in discursive and satirical poetry.

hovering stress (or accent). A term found in some textbooks, invented to deal with the problem of disyllabic feet in which the two syllables have equal stress-value, whether weak or strong. The argument in this book implies that this term should be rejected as a misleading confusion between stress value and metrical value.

hypermetrical. A term applied to a syllable which is not counted as part of the metre, usually occurring at the end of an iambic line to give a 'feminine' ending.

iambic. In addition to its use as a name for a metrical foot, this word sometimes appears in older literature with the meaning 'satirical'. This is a transferred meaning from the fact that the first appearance of iambic trimeter in Greek verse was as a vehicle for satire and invective. So Dryden advised Shadwell in *MacFlecknoe*:

> Thy Genius calls thee not to purchase fame
> In keen Iambicks, but mild Anagram.

ictus. The word means 'beat' and has been variously used in prosodic discussion to mean main stress, or main stress as indicator of the metrical accent, or the metrical accent itself. It is not used in this book.

numbers. In older usage the word was applied either to metrical feet, or to lines of verse, as in Pope's claim:

I lisp'd in Numbers, for the Numbers came.

onomatopoeia. Usually classified as a 'figure of speech', the term is connected with versification because it means the use of metrical and phonetic means to 'imitate the sense'.

ottava rima. A stanza of Italian origin consisting of eight iambic pentameter lines rhymed abababcc.

Pindaric ode. Pindar's odes have been imitated in English in a regular and an irregular form. The regular form is organized in three sections, each of which has three large stanzas: the strophe, the antistrophe, and the epode (or as Ben Jonson englished these choric terms, the turn, the counter-turn, the stand). The lines are of uneven length, but the strope and antistrophe keep the same form, while the epode is different. The irregular form, initiated by Cowley, does not observe these rules, and also changes its metre at will.

poulter's measure. A couplet formed by an iambic hexameter and an iambic heptameter rhyming together, frequently used in the sixteenth century. It broke down into 'short metre' (See *quatrain.*)

prosody. The study of versification, also called *metrics.* In a secondary sense it applies also to any particular system of versification, e.g. Greek prosody.

pyrrhic. A Classical quantitative foot consisting of two shorts. The attempt to introduce an analogous foot into English metre rests on a confusion between stress and accent. (See *hovering accent,* and *spondee,* and the discussion in the text.)

quantity. The duration of a vowel or a syllable. In Classical metres the pattern was based on assigning a quantitative value to every syllable in accordance with certain rules. In English, duration of vowels and syllables is artistically important but of no metrical significance.

quatrain. A four-line stanza. Special names have been acquired by some quatrains. The *heroic* or *elegiac quatrain* consists of iambic pentameters rhymed abab. *Ballad metre* is iambic tetrameter, trimeter, tetrameter, trimeter, usually rhymed abcb. Hymn forms also received special names: *common metre,* which is the same as ballad metre, or 'eights-and-sixes'; *long metre*, which is iambic tetrameters; *short metre*, which is trimeter, trimeter, tetrameter, trimeter.

rhyme. The standard type of rhyme is a combination of assonance and alliteration: it is the agreement of two metrically accented syllables in their vowel sounds and their terminal consonants. If there are unaccented syllables following the accented syllable, these must be identical. Agreement must not in English extend to the initial consonant or consonants: time/thyme is not acceptable in English though identical rhymes are favoured in French verse. By convention some words which formerly were exact rhymes in English are commonly admitted though pronunciation has shifted: one/alone, gone/done. Other imperfect rhymes are not infrequently used, either as liberties, or, in modern poetry, by a general intention to use near-rhyme. In sixteenth and seventeenth century discussions, the word 'rhyme' is sometimes used in a confusing way to mean 'rhythm' or 'verse', through a pedantic wish to bring the word back to its origin in the Latin word *rhythmus*, in turn derived from the Greek. Thus Milton, in the prologue to Book I of *Paradise Lost*, says his blank-verse epic will pursue :

Things unattempted yet in Prose or Rhime.

Terminal rhyme can have a structural value as indicating the endings of lines and the organization of stanzas.

rhyme royal. A seven-line stanza of iambic pentameters rhymed ababbcc, introduced by Chaucer but given the name 'royal' from its use by James I of Scotland.

rhythm. The word originates from the Greek word for 'flow'. It is best applied as a general term for the movement of verse as determined by metre, stress, pauses, pace.

sestina. A form of poem of Provençal origin, in which the terminal words of each line of the first stanza are repeated in a different order in the other stanzas. It consists of five stanzas with six lines each, concluding with a tornado of three lines in which all six repeated words occur in a middle or end position. The lines are usually iambic pentameters. The standard order of repetitions is: 1,2,3,4,5,6—6,1,5,2,4,3—3,6,4,1,2,5—5,3,2,6,1,4—4,5,1,3,6,2—2,4,6,5,3,1—concluding 2/5, 4/3, 6/1. The form is occasionally used in contemporary poetry.

sonnet. In the strict sense, a fourteen-line poem usually in iambic pentameters. The Italian or Petrarchan type consists of an octet, usually rhymed abba abba, and a sestet rhymed cde cde or in some permutation of these. The English type consists of three quatrains plus a concluding couplet, rhymed variously, the Shakespearian form being abab cdcd efef gg. In sixteenth and seventeenth century use, the term was also loosely applied to any lyric poem, especially a love-poem, as in Donne's *Songs and Sonets*.

Spenserian Stanza. A nine-line stanza used in *The Faerie Queene*, consisting of eight iambic pentameters followed by an iambic hexameter (alexandrine) and rhymed ababbcbcc.

spondee. The same objection applies to the attempt to introduce this foot into English scansion as to *pyrrhic (q.v.)*

sprung rhythm. The name given by Gerard Manley Hopkins to his scheme of accentual versification.

stanza. A group of four or more lines, usually with a fixed rhyme-scheme, though not invariably. The Italian word also means 'a room'; whence Donne's punning line in 'The Canonization':

> We'll build in Sonnets pretty roomes.

syllable. Linguistic theorists disagree about the definition of the syllable, its demarcation, and whether it is a true unit for metrical purposes. However it seems satisfactory to say that a syllable is precisely that which bears stress and invites a metrical value. A convenient rule is to divide syllables thus: ma/ker, mas/ter.

tercet. A set of three lines, often but not necessarily rhymed aaa, also called a triplet.

terza rima. A verse form of Italian origin, consisting of sets of three iambic pentameters with interlocking rhymes: aba bcb cdc, and so on.

A SELECT LIST FOR READING

A. D. Hope, 'Free Verse: A Post Mortem', in *The Cave and the Spring*, Adelaide, Rigby, 1965.

A discussion of the nature of traditional verse as a basis for a critical comment on free verse and *vers libéré*.

Catherine Ing, *Elizabethan Lyrics*, London, Chatto and Windus, 1951.

Contains observations of general interest as well as a study of Elizabethan metrical theory and practice.

C. S. Lewis, 'Metre', *A Review of English Literature*, Vol. 1, No. 1, 1960.

A short and sensible plea for the traditional method of scansion.

George Saintsbury, *A History of English Prosody* (3 vols.), London, Macmillan, 1906-10.

A mine of information and vigorous discussion, representing a great advance on some of the aberrant theorizing of the time, but not fully satisfactory as an exposition of metrical principles.

John Thompson, *The Founding of English Metre*, London, Routledge and Kegan Paul, 1961.

Primarily an historical account of the evolution of verse from Wyatt to Sidney, but the Introduction is one of the best short treatments of the subject available.

Yvor Winters, *In Defense of Reason*, London, Routledge and Kegan Paul, 1960.

Contains a penetrating exposition of traditional versification, and an analysis of some modern alternatives.